D0008511

LIFE IN THE KINGDOM

JACK W. HAYFORD

NELSON REFERENCE & ELECTRONIC
A Division of Thomas Nelson Publishers
Since 1798

www.thomasnelson.com

Spirit-Filled Life® Study Guide: Life in the Kingdom

Copyright © 2004 by Jack W. Hayford

Printed in Nashville, Tennessee, by Thomas Nelson, Inc.

Library of Congress Cataloging-in-Publication Data is available.

Hayford, Jack W.

Life in the Kingdom

ISBN 0-7852-4987-7

Printed in the United States of America

1 2 3 4 5 6 7—09 08 07 06 05 04

CONTENTS

Introduction:
The Kingdom and You
Part One

Jesus Christ tells the story of a wise person who built his house on a solid foundation and contrasts that with a person who used a sandy foundation. During a raging storm, the house of the person who heeded Jesus' teaching held steady, but the one that had no foundation in Jesus collapsed (Matt. 7:24-27).

Just as rains and wind tested the houses where those two people lived, so today, we need a solid foundation to weather the storms of adverse circumstances, the winds of false teaching, and the floods of unrighteousness that characterize the times in which we live. That solid foundation is Jesus.

Understanding and acting on the central core of His message as the King of the heavenly kingdom will stabilize and solidify your faith. It will secure your life and strengthen everything of your experience, your family, your business, and your witness, whatever the circumstances. If the foundation of your faith is solid, you need not fear! Your life will stand on the solid foundation of the eternal Word of God.

The Kingdom Is for Today

With powerful yet tender words, Jesus comforts us and proclaims a transforming truth that was central to everything He taught: "Do not fear, little flock, for it is your Father's good pleasure to give you the kingdom" (Luke 12:32).

What does the "kingdom of God" mean? Is it as important today as it was when Jesus spoke of it? Be assured, life in the kingdom and the foundations of our faith are integrally related, and to understand what it means to live in the kingdom of God is vital in establishing a solid foundation for your faith NOW!

A study of the Bible's teaching about the kingdom of God and what it means to live in this kingdom is a way of allowing the Scripture's intended purpose to be fulfilled in your life. It is a way of allowing the Word of God to strengthen the foundation of your faith and to reach out to a desperate world with Holy Spirit-given power. You will discover that the kingdom of God is *accessible* because of Father God's gift of Jesus, and it is *livable* because of the gift of His Holy Spirit.

THE KINGDOM CALLS YOU!

As we begin, come straight to the Word and listen to seven kingdom trumpet calls! They boldly resound the heart, the preaching, and the actions of our Lord Jesus Christ.

1. Jesus' first public proclamation was, "Repent, for the kingdom of heaven is at hand" (Matt. 4:17).
2. Jesus claimed He was sent by His Father to "preach the kingdom of God" (Luke 4:43).
3. Jesus taught His disciples to pray to their heavenly Father, "Your kingdom come. Your will be done on earth as it is in heaven" (Matt. 6:10).
4. Jesus told them to "seek first the kingdom of God and His righteousness" (Matt. 6:33).
5. Jesus promised them the kingdom belonged to "the poor in spirit" and to those who are "persecuted for righteousness' sake" (Matt. 5:3, 10).
6. He assured them that although they would be "hated by all nations for My name's sake . . . this gospel of the kingdom will be preached in all the world as a witness to all the nations, and then the end will come" (Matt. 24:9, 14).
7. During His last forty days before His return to heaven, Jesus spoke to His disciples about "the things pertaining to the kingdom of God" (Acts 1:3).

FAITH ALIVE

Hearing and doing the Word is the way a wise person builds on the "Rock" of Jesus Christ. So get your Bible, and let's anticipate this exciting and essential adventure of building foundational, kingdom-of-God truth into your life! The kingdom of God is at hand!

KINGDOM ACCESS
Lesson One

THE BIG IDEA

"The kingdom of God is at hand." This life-changing truth was at the heart of Jesus' ministry. What exactly is the kingdom of God? How can you enter it? Discover how the King and His kingdom can transform your life!

WHAT IS THE KINGDOM?

The kingdom is centered in the King. Through Jesus Christ, that which God the Father intended from the beginning will happen: God's kingdom will come and His will will be done on earth as it is in heaven (Luke 11:2). Jesus came to

1. Release us from the bondage of self, sin, sickness, and Satan;
2. Restore relationship with God;
3. Restore what man lost in the Fall;
4. Lay the foundation through His Cross for the release of all other blessings, including kingdom life and ministry.

The implications of the kingdom are enormous. *Because our redemption has been fully accomplished in Jesus, we can experience the life and power of God's kingdom in the present, while still anticipating the kingdom's final fullness and consummation in the future.* We who are Christ's are His kingdom people! He calls us to live like His children! And until He returns, God's ministry will flow in us to touch a broken world with His power and glory.

SALVATION THROUGH THE KING
(Luke 19:10; 1 Tim. 2:4–6)

As we dig into Scripture throughout this study guide, we will see that the kingdom of God is near, and it is available. This is good news! Let's start by investigating the purpose for which Jesus was sent.

◈ What did the angel say to Joseph about Jesus' purpose? (Matt. 1:21)

_____

_____

_____

◈ How did the announcement of the angel to the shepherds at the birth of Jesus confirm this purpose? (Luke 2:11)

_____

_____

_____

◈ God is a saving God. Describe the content of these two verses as they show what Jesus' foundational ministry was to provide:

Luke 19:10 _____

_____

_____

1 Timothy 2:4–6 _____

_____

_____

The foundational ministry of the kingdom is the ministry of salvation. But within salvation's full provision are deliverance, release, and liberation from all that prevents God's will from being accomplished. The coming of the kingdom is to bring about the fulfillment of God's saving purposes for humankind, that we might live "to the praise of His glory" (Eph. 1:12). The saving ministry of the kingdom in the life of our Savior, Jesus Christ, is overflowing with love and grace to bring praise and glory to God through His manifest works in us.

Salvation is so much more than getting to heaven someday! A study of New Testament Greek words for "salvation" is fascinating. Read the Word Wealth definitions and write your own definition of salvation.

WORD WEALTH

Salvation, *soteria* (Luke 19:9). Deliverance, preservation, soundness, prosperity, happiness, rescue, general well-being. The word is used both in a material, temporal sense and in a spiritual, eternal sense. The New Testament especially uses the word for spiritual well-being. Salvation is a present possession (Luke 1:77; 2 Cor. 1:6; 7:10) with a fuller realization in the future (Rom. 13:11; 1 Thess. 5:8, 9).

Salvation, *soterion* (Acts 28:28). Rescue, deliverance, safety, liberation, release, preservation, and the general word for Christian salvation. *Soterion* only occurs five times. *Soteria*, the generic word, occurs forty-five times. It is an all-inclusive word signifying forgiveness, healing, prosperity, deliverance, safety, rescue, liberation, and restoration. Christ's salvation is total in scope for the total man: spirit, soul, and body.

◈ My definition of salvation:

_____

_____

_____

_____

HOW TO ENTER THE KINGDOM (MARK 1:14, 15)

The gospel message of both John the Baptist and Jesus started with a proclamation of the nearness of the kingdom of God, introducing to humankind a new era of salvation.

◈ Turn to Mark 1:14, 15. What does Jesus say?

_____

_____

◈ What two things does a person need to do to enter the kingdom? (v. 15)

_____

_____

Unfortunately, our culture has diluted our understanding of repentance as well as belief in the Lord Jesus Christ. Let's briefly study the meaning of these two essential prerequisites for entering God's kingdom. We will start with repentance.

WORD WEALTH

Repent, *metanoeo* (Matt. 3:2). From *meta*, "after," and *noeo*, meaning "to think." Repentance is a decision that results in a change of mind, which in turn leads to a change of purpose and action.

Briefly stated, repentance can be described as an internal sorrow that results in turning—forsaking former attitudes and/or behaviors and embracing new ones that align with God's Spirit and His Word. Truly, there is no birth into the kingdom without hearing the call to salvation, renouncing one's sin, and turning from sin toward Christ the Savior.

◈ What is the difference between true repentance and being sorry you got caught?

_____

_____

_____

_____

_____

_____

◈ Using the definitions to help you, write what repentance really means.

_____

_____

_____

_____

FAITH ALIVE

Is there an area of your life right now for which you need to repent? If so, why not do that? As you do, know that repentance leads you to a relationship with God.

WORD WEALTH

Believe, *pisteuo* (Rom. 10:9). The verb form of *pistis*, "faith." It means to trust in, have faith in, be fully convinced of, acknowledge, rely on. *Pisteuo* is more than credence in church doctrines or articles of faith. It expresses reliance upon and a personal trust that produces obedience. It includes submission and a positive confession of the lordship of Jesus.

Believing includes both acceptance and adherence. In reference to a person, to believe means both to accept that which is true about the individual and to commit oneself personally in light of such information. Thus, to believe in Jesus Christ means both to accept as true that which is said about Him and, in light of such information, to fully rely and trust Him as expressed in obedience to His words.

◈ What is the difference between mentally assenting to a certain belief and wholly adhering to it?

_____

_____

◈ Why do you think repentance and believing in God are essential for entrance into the kingdom of God?

_____

_____

_____

FAITH ALIVE

Describe what your belief in Jesus Christ means to you.

_____

_____

_____

_____

_____

_____

_____

NEW BIRTH
(John 3:1–16)

Jesus said that to see the kingdom of God one must be born again, not through a second biological birth but by spiritual birth. This birth dramatically indicates three things:

1. Without new birth, there is no life and no relationship with God (John 14:6).
2. In new birth, new perspective comes as we "see the kingdom of God" (John 3:3). God's Word becomes clear, and the Holy Spirit's works and wonders are believed and experienced.
3. Through new birth we are introduced—literally we "enter" (John 3:5)—to a new realm, where God's new kingdom order can be realized (2 Cor. 5:17).

New birth is more than simply being saved for heaven someday. It is a requalifying experience, opening up the possibilities of our whole being to the supernatural dimension of life and fitting us for a beginning in God's kingdom order.

◇ Read the entire passage of John 3:1–16. Why did Jesus say a person must be born again to see the kingdom of God?

_____

_____

_____

_____

◇ How would you explain the new birth to a non-believer?

_____

_____

◇ In Matthew 18:3, Jesus talked about the heart attitude of a person coming to God for new birth. What did He say, and why do you think He said it?

_____

_____

Entrance into the kingdom requires a complete change from the way the world views greatness and life. So different is God's kingdom from human kingdoms that nothing less than rebirth through humble repentance and faith will gain us entrance. Good works—whether proper confession, mighty ministry, or religious position—are to no avail. All our "righteousnesses" are like filthy rags" (Is. 64:6). We must experience something entirely new. We must be "born of water and the Spirit" (John 3:5).

FAITH ALIVE

Repenting and believing are not mere mental exercises. As we completely turn from sin and fully trust the Good News about Jesus Christ, we discover that the kingdom of God is "at hand." We are born again. In your devotional time, focus on the nearness of the King and His kingdom to you.

ARE "KINGDOM OF HEAVEN" AND "KINGDOM OF GOD" THE SAME?
(Matt. 19:23, 24)

The terms *kingdom of God*, *kingdom of heaven*, and *kingdom* appear frequently in the Gospels (117 times in the synoptic Gospels and five times in John). Of the occurrences in the Gospels, about one hundred are found on the lips of Jesus Himself. Elsewhere in the New Testament, references to the kingdom occur thirty-three times.

◇ If Jesus spoke of the kingdom of God a hundred times, what does that tell you of the importance of the kingdom to Him?

_____

_____

_____

_____

_____

You may have noticed that we have used "kingdom of heaven" and the "kingdom of God" interchangeably. It is important for you to see that these are synonymous expressions in the Bible.

◈ Turn to Matthew 19:23, 24. In this conversation about entering the kingdom, note the two terms for the kingdom that Jesus uses. What are those terms and how does Jesus use them?

_____

_____

_____

_____

_____

KINGDOM EXTRA

Although some make a labored distinction between the "kingdom of heaven" and the "kingdom of God," this text (Matt. 19:23, 24) and ten others in the Gospels clearly show that the two terms are verifiably synonyms.

Matthew is the only New Testament writer who used the term "kingdom of heaven." Why did he do that? It is highly probable that Matthew was showing a sensitivity toward his originally intended audience of Jewish readers, for whom too frequent a use of the name of "God" would have seemed irreverent. By a variety of terms, Matthew refers to "the kingdom" fifty times in his Gospel: thirty-two times as "kingdom of heaven"; five times as "kingdom of God"; four times as the "Father's" kingdom; and twice as the kingdom of "the Son of Man." The remaining seven references are simply to "the kingdom" without other designation. This variety in the usage, made by the only one using the phrase "kingdom of heaven," surely shows these terms to be synonyms for the kingdom.

THE KINGDOM INVITES YOUR RESPONSE
(Matt. 13:3–9, 18–23)

In the well-known parable of the sower, Jesus communicated what happens when people hear the word of the kingdom.

◈ Look at each of the four different places where the seeds landed in Matthew 13. Then write the result in terms of harvest and what each means.

Places where the seeds landed:	What happened? (vv. 4–8)	What does it mean? (vv. 18–23)
By the wayside		
On stony places		
Among the thorns		
On good ground		

◇ Note that in every case, the seed that was planted was the same: it was the condition of the soil that determined the result. Such is the case with the kingdom of God—there are various kinds of receptivity to the Word. How should one who has "ears to hear" respond to this truth (vv. 9, 18)?

_____

_____

_____

_____

Jesus is saying that the condition of the soil of your heart is reflected by your willingness to hear what the Holy Spirit is seeking to communicate to you about Christ's life and purpose. The overarching truth is that the personal impact of God's sovereign kingdom power is determined by human response. God's kingdom can be rejected, temporarily accepted, or fully and fruitfully accepted. This parable vividly pictures the varied response to Jesus' proclamation of the word of the kingdom—from the hardened hearers, to the temporarily responsive multitudes, to the receptive disciples.

The same is true today. God's kingdom rule can be resisted or received! The same seed of the word can have such dramatically different outcomes—like the sun, which both hardens clay and softens wax!

FAITH ALIVE

◇ How can you ensure that the "soil" of your life is receptive to God's reign?

_____

_____

_____

◇ What situations in your life need to be touched by God's kingdom?

_____

_____

_____

THE KINGDOM'S KING
Lesson 2

THE BIG IDEA

The best news of the kingdom is the King Himself! Let's study the person and work of our King, the Lord Jesus Christ, who redeems and restores us.

JESUS' MISSION
(Matt. 4:23, 24; Acts 1:3)

Jesus clearly understood His identity as well as His mission. Both led Him to the Cross. Let's start with the purpose for which He was sent.

◇ What did Jesus preach? (Matt. 4:23)

_____

_____

◇ What did Jesus do? (Matt. 4:23, 24)

_____

_____

◇ What is the relationship between these two activities? Are both needed? Why?

_____

_____

◇ If Jesus' purpose was to declare and demonstrate God's kingdom, what kind of a kingdom is it? Why is it called "Good News"?

_____

_____

_____

◈ Turn to Acts 1:3. What did Jesus teach after His Resurrection?

_____

_____

The Bible says that Jesus did so many things that the world could not "contain the books that would be written" about Him (John 21:25). Jesus came to

1. Release humankind from the bondage of self, sin, sickness, and Satan;
2. Restore what man lost in the Fall;
3. Restore relationship with God;
3. Lay the foundation through His Cross for the release of all other blessings, including kingdom ministry.

Truly, it is wonderful news that Jesus Christ made it possible for us to experience all the blessings of the kingdom. Jesus both *brings* and *models* God's sovereign rule!

FAITH ALIVE

As you begin this lesson, allow the Holy Spirit to reveal Jesus to you in a new or different way. As you do, take a situation in your life needing freedom from sin, self, sickness, or Satan. Let "I will see Jesus in this," be your heart's cry, and wait on Him to see what He will do!

JESUS, THE ROYAL SON OF DAVID

Next, as we dig deeper into the identity of Jesus, it is important to look at the three titles used most frequently for Jesus in the Gospels—the royal Son of David, the servant Son of Man, and the divine Son of God. He is all three, and much more!

Let's look at the first title, the Son of David. The exciting thing is that this name was prophesied centuries before Jesus was born as the Son of David. In the Jewish culture to which Jesus came, the most widely held view of the Messiah was that of a descendant of King David who would inherit his kingly rule. The Gospel of Matthew underscores this view with its opening: "genealogy of Jesus Christ, the Son of David, the Son of Abraham" (1:1). Matthew's purpose here was to proclaim Jesus' royal lineage (Son of David) and His link with the founder of the Jewish people (Son of Abraham). In addition, Matthew wanted to demonstrate the continuity between Jesus and the Israel of the Old Testament.

Look up the following verses from the first four chapters in Matthew and write down what Old Testament messianic promise that was fulfilled by Christ's coming.

Matthew 1:23 / Isaiah 7:14

_____

_____

Matthew 2:5, 6 / Micah 5:2

_____

_____

Matthew 2:15 / Hosea 11:1

_____

_____

Matthew 2:18 / Jeremiah 31:15

_____

_____

Matthew 2:23 / Isaiah 11:1

_____

_____

Matthew 3:3 / Isaiah 40:3

_____

_____

Matthew 4:14–16 / Isaiah 9:1, 2

_____

_____

Kingdom Extra

Direct quotations from the Old Testament in the New have been numbered around 250. When allusions are added, the total rises to more than 600. (Some have even calculated the total to be as high as 4,000.) Such frequent use of the Old Testament in the New illustrates the understanding that the events of the life of Jesus Christ and the church reflect a period of prophetic fulfillment. The wide variation in the numbering of such usage indicates the diversity with which New Testament writers used Old Testament passages.

The seven fulfillment quotations that we just looked at illustrate such variation. In some cases the application is quite similar to the original historical setting (Matt. 2:5, 6 and Mic. 5:2). But in other cases, the application seems quite different from the setting in the Old Testament. For example, Hosea's reference to the Exodus of Israel as "fulfilled" in Jesus' return from Egypt is interesting (Matt. 2:15). And in still other cases one wonders what passage the writer had in mind (Matt. 2:23: "He shall be called a Nazarene"). What are we to make of all this? Misquotation? Misinterpretation? Allegorization? Spiritualization? Probably the answers are to be found in a proper understanding of the nature of "fulfillment." It does not necessarily mean "exact duplication." More likely it means practical and real "expanded application." The basic issue is the "filling full" of the original passage. Thus, the "filling full" of the Immanuel passage in Isaiah 7:14 about Jesus' Virgin Birth (quoted in Matt. 1:23) goes far beyond the original historical context. Just as the "filling full" of an acorn is an oak tree (not another acorn.), so the "filling full" of "God with us" is the birth of God's Son, not another human being like Isaiah's son. Classic books which have proven helpful on this question are: E. Earle Ellis's *Paul's Use of the Old Testament* (Eerdmans, 1957) and R. V. G. Tasker's *The Old Testament in the New Testament* (SCM Press, 1946).

Yes, the Gospel of Matthew clearly indicates Jesus was the Davidic Messiah. But Matthew also clearly indicates that Jesus understood His Davidic messiahship in a way different from that of the popular conception. Thus, Jesus pointedly asked His disciples not only "Who do men say that I ... am?" but "Who do you say that I am?"

1. Matthew 16:13–16

Who did men say Jesus was? (v. 14)

_____

_____

_____

Who did Peter say Jesus was? (v. 16)

_____

_____

_____

2. Matthew 16:17–20

Who does Jesus say revealed to Peter the true identity of Jesus? (v. 17)

_____

_____

_____

Why do you think verse 20 says that Jesus "commanded His disciples that they should tell no one that He was Jesus the Christ"? (Christ means "Messiah.")

_____

_____

_____

3. Matthew 16:21–23

Notice both Peter's reaction to Jesus' words about His death and Jesus' response to Peter's reaction. What does this reaction indicate about the disciples' understanding of the nature of Jesus' messiahship?

_____

_____

_____

_____

Why was dying incompatible with the disciples' view of the Messiah?

_____

_____

_____

_____

4. Matthew 22:41–45

To drive home the point about the true nature of His Davidic messiahship, Jesus posed a perplexing question for the Pharisees. What was Jesus' point?

_____

_____

_____

Yes, Jesus claimed to be the "son-of-David" Messiah, but with a difference. Jesus was a different kind of Messiah and King. He was divine, the Lord, the King. But rather than coming to wield His authority to rule as was expected, He came to serve.

JESUS, THE SERVANT SON OF MAN

"Son of Man" was the title Jesus preferred to use of Himself. The Gospels record it on His lips more than sixty-five times.

◈ Jesus' use of "Son of Man" is fascinating. Look at the first part of Mark 10:45. Why did the "Son of Man" come?

_____

_____

_____

_____

A careful study of Mark's Gospel will reveal that it focuses on Jesus as servant. Mark offers no genealogy, as Matthew and Luke do. Who wants to know the family background of a servant? In contrast to Matthew, the focus in Mark is more on Jesus' miracles than on His teaching. It is the Gospel of action, for servants are better known for their deeds than for their words! And so, the "Son of Man" healed the sick, cast out demons, fed the multitudes, and raised the dead. Indeed, Jesus Christ came to serve others, not Himself.

It is interesting to note the times when Jesus seemed to use the title "Son of Man." Frequently He used it when He encountered misunderstanding as to who He was—especially by the unbelieving religious leaders.

Look up these passages and discover the point of misunderstanding:

Matthew 12:32

_____

_____

Mark 2:10, 11

_____

_____

Mark 2:27, 28

_____

_____

Luke 7:34

_____

_____

Luke 19:10

_____

_____

Now, look at the second part of Mark 10:45. What did Jesus' call to serve involve?

_____

_____

_____

Let's study what this important word—"ransom"—means.

WORD WEALTH

Ransom, *lutron* (Matt. 20:28). From the verb *luo,* "to loose." The word signifies a release from slavery or captivity brought about by the payment of a price. Sin demands an expiation, an atonement, a price paid because of the penalty of death that was upon us. Jesus' gift to us was Himself, a universal ransom (for many) that was of a vicarious nature. *Lutron* defines the price paid canceling our debt.

◈ What does sin demand?

_____

_____

_____

◈ Who met the demand and paid the price for our release? What does that mean?

_____

_____

_____

Now, let's go back to Peter's confession of Jesus as Messiah in Matthew 16:13–21. Note that Jesus used the title "Son of Man" in verse 13 to describe Himself. Then in verse 21 Jesus begins to teach something He apparently had not clearly taught prior to that time—that He would be killed. This incident is a hinge point in Jesus' revelation of the true nature of His messiahship: it will involve crucifixion! From that time on, the "Son of Man" title will be connected with suffering and death.

In John 12:32–34, Jesus clearly tied His role as Messiah to suffering. In so doing, He linked Old Testament passages which before had never been tied together—namely, Isaiah 9:6, 7 and Isaiah 52:13—53:12 passages. Look these up and describe the distinguishing differences in the role of the One being foretold.

John 12:32–34 _____

_____

_____

Isaiah 9:6, 7 _____

_____

_____

_____

Isaiah 52:13—53:12 _____

_____

_____

_____

Most significantly, the suffering "Son of Man" is to be honored with great glory. Jesus clearly taught He was the "Son of Man" who would come in power and great glory like the prophet Daniel predicted (Matt. 26:64; Dan. 7:13). Thus, it appeared Jesus deliberately chose to use the title "Son of Man" to teach the true nature of His messiahship, linking suffering and ruling. Thereby, He was able to take a largely unknown title and fill it with new meaning about the true nature of His mission as Messiah. He would fulfill His messianic role through dying and rising. This would be the basis of the forgiveness of sins to be proclaimed to all nations. True deliverance from sin's tyranny required sin's penalty be paid and sin's power broken. God's kingdom rule required, first and foremost, the breaking of sin's rule. And that is why Jesus came as a suffering Servant to die on our behalf and rise again.

FAITH ALIVE

Most people recognize that a ransom is an amount paid in exchange for a kidnapped person. It "buys back" the person. In the biblical context, it means so much more! In your own words, write about how Jesus' paying your ransom with His life applies to your relationship with God. Use what "ransom" means in Scripture and what you learned of Jesus' purpose in His role as "Son of Man" to help develop your answer.

JESUS, THE DIVINE SON OF GOD

Jesus' identity is clearly linked to His relationship with God as His Father. Many thought that it was presumptuous to claim such a truth, and it evoked violent reaction from the religious leaders of His day. It was this perceived blasphemy that caused them to want to put Jesus to death (Matt. 26:65, 66).

For each of the passages, write what it says about Jesus and His relationship to God the Father.

Matthew 26:63, 64 _____

_____

_____

Luke 22:67–71 _____

_____

_____

John 5:18

John 10:30

John 14:9, 10

More than one hundred times Jesus referred to God as "Father" in the Gospel of John. The religious leaders knew exactly what Jesus was saying each time that He called God His Father! Further, He constantly used the divine name revealed to Moses—"I AM"—to describe Himself and define His mission as God's anointed Messiah sent to accomplish redemption.

Look up the following passages and identify what Jesus said about Himself that applies to God alone:

John 8:12; 9:5

John 8:58; 18:5, 6

John 10:7, 9

John 10:11, 14

John 14:7

_____

_____

_____

_____

The message is clear. Jesus Christ is the Son of God. In fact that is why John wrote his Gospel—that we might believe that "Jesus is the Christ, the Son of God," and that believing we would have "life in His name" (John 20:31).

WE WOULD SEE JESUS
(John 20:24–31)

Jesus' disciple, Thomas, had been with Jesus throughout His ministry. Thomas had heard His teachings, seen the miracles, shared bread with Him—in short, Thomas knew Jesus well. And yet, Thomas doubted that Jesus had risen from the dead, which essentially meant he doubted the claims of Jesus as the Son of God.

In order to encourage Thomas to believe, Jesus invited Thomas to put his hand in His torn side and his finger in the nailprints of His hands. When Thomas finally came face to face with the reality of Jesus as God, he came to the end of his doubts and said, "My Lord and my God!" (John 20:28). May we also come to the same conclusion!

FAITH ALIVE
_____

You may have known the Lord for a short while; you may be a mature believer who has been with Him for a long time. Or you may have heard about Him but never have come to know Him personally. Whatever your situation, ask for a fresh encounter of the reality of Jesus in your life! Be encouraged because Jesus told Thomas, "Because you have seen Me, you have believed. Blessed are those who have not seen and yet have believed" (John 20:29).

IMPACT OF THE KINGDOM

Lesson 3

THE BIG IDEA

How do we describe a sunset to a blind person or the music of Bach to a deaf person? In God's kingdom, we experience realities beyond our senses. We walk by faith, not by sight. As you live in the kingdom, you will discover that it is far brighter and richer than you ever could imagine!

THE VALUE AND COST OF THE KINGDOM
(Matt. 13:44–46; Mark 8:34–38)

The value of the kingdom is priceless! It is so precious that a person who sees the kingdom will be willing to give everything to share in it.

◇ Read Matthew 13:44. What is the kingdom of heaven likened to?

_____

_____

_____

◇ What motivated the person to sell all he had? (v. 44)

_____

_____

_____

◇ Read Matthew 13:45, 46. What is the kingdom of heaven likened to here?

_____

_____

_____

◇ What did the person find? What did he do about it? (v. 46)

_____

_____

_____

Entrance into the kingdom requires a complete reorientation of values and priorities, for it is a call to life-changing discipleship.

◇ Look up Mark 8:34. What three things did Jesus say a person needs to do to follow Him?

_____

_____

_____

◇ Now look at verses 35–38. What does Jesus require?

_____

_____

_____

The demand of the kingdom was unparalleled. But so was the price in making this blessed kingdom available. If it would cost Jesus everything to bring God's kingdom to humankind, could it cost people any less to enter it and enjoy its blessings? Of course not! Thus, the demand of the kingdom required a resolute, radical, costly, and eternal decision.

◇ Discipleship calls for decision! For each type of decision, write down the illustration(s) Jesus used and the point He was teaching.

Decision	Illustration(s)	Point
A resolute decision (Luke 9:57–62)		
A radical decision (Luke 14:25, 26)		

Decision	Illustration(s)	Point
A costly decision (Luke 14:26, 27)		
An eternal decision (John 3:16)		

It is important to realize what we receive when we give our all to God. It is true that taking up our cross daily provokes a confrontation with the human tendency to pursue our own will, way, and wants. But even as Jesus laid down His life for us, He invites us to lay down ours for His. It is not an equal exchange. He died to do for us what we could never do for ourselves—to save us and give us eternal life. But when we sacrifice for Him, that opens the way for His life to reveal even more of the glory of His way and will—to discover new dimensions of eternal love and liberty that bring freedom from bondage to our self-life.

FAITH ALIVE

Weigh the differences between the cost of discipleship and the rich value of discipleship in your life. As you follow Jesus, what blessings can you receive? As you evaluate what following the Father cost Jesus, seek to determine what discipleship costs you.

THE KINGDOM IS DIFFERENT THAN IT SEEMS

In studying this great theme, the great challenge is to understand what Jesus meant by the word *kingdom*. What Jesus meant by the word and what His "contemporaries" popularly understood were not necessarily the same.

◇ Look up the following passages and write down the contrast between the popular understanding and Jesus' understanding of the kingdom.

Scriptures	Popular Understanding	Jesus Understanding
Luke 17:20, 21		
John 6:10–15, 26		
John 18:10, 11, 36		
Acts 1:6, 7		

◇ Where do you think the Jews got their nationalistic understanding of the kingdom?

_____

_____

◇ How did Jesus receive His understanding of the kingdom?

_____

_____

◇ If former Jewish prophets and kings had seen the ministry of the kingdom, what do you think they would have thought about it? (Luke 10:24)

_____

_____

It is clear that Jesus' understanding of the kingdom was not the same as the popular conception. His kingdom had to do more with *spiritual* than political liberation. It had more to do with *authority* than territory.

AUTHORITY IN THE KINGDOM, NOW!
(Matt. 10:1–8; 28:18; Luke 10:1–19; Acts 1:7, 8)

Jesus operated with kingdom authority. He *had* authority because He operated *under* His Father's authority.

◇ What did the people recognize about Jesus when He taught in the synagogue? How was this different from the scribes? (Mark 1:22)

_____

_____

◇ What insight to God's authority and power did the Roman centurion declare in Luke 7:8?

_____

_____

Look at a Greek word for authority, *exousia*, sometimes translated "power."

WORD WEALTH

Power, *exousia* (Mark 3:15). One of four power words (*dunamis, exousia, ischus,* and *kratos*), *exousia* means the authority or right to act, ability, privilege, capacity, delegated authority. Jesus had the *exousia* to forgive sin, heal sicknesses, and cast out devils. *Exousia* is the right to use *dunamis,* "might." Jesus gave His followers *exousia* to preach, teach, heal, and deliver (Mark 3:15), and that authority has never been rescinded (John 14:12). Powerless ministries become powerful upon discovering the *exousia* power that is resident in the name of Jesus and the blood of Jesus.

◇ Look up both verses cited in this Word Wealth and summarize what they say.

_____

_____

_____

Because Jesus came only to do the will of His Father, the liberating rule of God was released when He spoke. People were set free! In the following passages, Jesus spoke with the liberating authority of His Father. Look at each passage and list what the people were freed from.

Mark 1:23–26

_____

_____

Mark 2:3–12

_____

_____

Mark 4:35–41

_____

_____

_____

The amazing fact of kingdom authority is that Jesus delegated it to His disciples. This is what kingdom ministry is all about! When Jesus sent the Twelve out to preach the kingdom of heaven, He gave them "power" (_exousia_), saying, "Freely you have received, freely give" (Matt. 10:1, 7, 8; see also Mark 3:14, 15).

✧ What did Jesus give the disciples the power to do? (Matt. 10:1, 7, 8)

_____

_____

_____

Likewise, seventy others were sent out and also received powerful authority for ministry (Luke 10:1–9).

✧ What were they to say to the people who were healed? (v. 9)

_____

_____

_____

✧ Why were these disciples joyfully exuberant? (v. 17)

_____

_____

_____

Read Jesus' complete response to their enthusiasm in Luke 10:18–20.

◇ What event had Jesus witnessed? (v. 18)

_____

_____

◇ What kind of authority over the enemy has Jesus imparted to His followers? (v. 19)

_____

_____

◇ Are we to "rejoice" in our God-granted authority or in our salvation? (v. 20)

_____

_____

These two episodes introduced Jesus' followers to the awesome privilege of kingdom ministry in kingdom power. Afterward, He gave His global "Great Commission" to His church for all time, to go and "make disciples of the nations" (Matt. 28:19, 20).

◇ What did Jesus say had been granted to Him in heaven and on earth? (Matt. 28: 18)

_____

_____

_____

◇ Note Jesus' use of "therefore" in verse 19. Explain the basis on which He gave this worldwide commission.

_____

_____

_____

The resurrected Christ had been given all-encompassing *exousia* (authority) "in heaven and in earth." His decisive victory over the kingdom of darkness was the basis of His commission to the nations. He had broken, once and for all, the power of death and hell. The world needed to know!

The Book of Acts records what happened when His disciples went in His authority and in His name powerfully preached Good News, declared forgiveness of sin, healed the sick, cast out demons, and raised the dead. They went in the power of the Spirit. Jesus said in Acts 1:7, 8, "It is not for you to know times or seasons which the Father has put in His own authority (*exousia*). But you shall receive power (*dunamis*) when the Holy Spirit has come upon you." Let's study the kind of power granted to the church, *dunamis*.

WORD WEALTH

Power, *dunamis* (Acts 4:33). Energy, power, might, great force, great ability, strength. It is sometimes used to describe the powers of the world to come at work upon the earth and divine power overcoming all resistance. (Compare "dynamic," "dynamite," and "dynamometer.") The *dunamis* in Jesus resulted in dramatic transformations. This is the norm for the Spirit-filled and Spirit-led church.

◇ Compare *dunamis* with the Word Wealth definition *exousia* (power) given earlier in this lesson. What is the difference between them?

_____

_____

◇ Look up these passages. When kingdom people move with God-given kingdom authority into kingdom ministry, what will happen?

Acts 1:8 _____

_____

_____

Acts 4:13 _____

_____

_____

Acts 4:33 _____

_____

_____

FAITH ALIVE

So many times, God's authority is misinterpreted. This is what is true about His authority:

1. God's authority is freeing, not oppressive.
2. It elicits our trust, not our fear.
3. It does not squash our individuality; it brings order to our lives.
4. It does not injure us; it brings us to a place under His leadership where we can be healed.

How are these different from popular notions of authority, and is God's authority the kind of authority you can accept? Write your thoughts on this subject.

GREATER WORKS
(John 14:12)

Before His death, Jesus told His disciples, "He who believes in Me, the works that I do he will do also; and greater works than these he will do, because I go to My Father" (John 14:12).

◇ Read John 14:10–14 and notice the context—believing and prayer. Write what Jesus says just before and after His promise of greater works (vv. 10–12a; 13, 14).

◇ Where is Jesus going that necessitates His giving of greater works? (John 14:12)

That you will do "greater works" than Jesus Himself is an astounding promise. Note that the verse doesn't say "*better* works," but "*greater* works." This means the works are on a wider scope: more healings, more exorcisms, more resurrections, because His witnesses have multiplied His ministry thousands of times over as they extended His kingdom rule from Jerusalem to the ends of the earth.

The Good News is that there is no "expiration date" on these "greater works"! The rapid and widespread growth of the Pentecostal and charismatic movement today is demonstrating that "greater works" are for people who simply believe and ask. More people are believing and asking than ever before!

Like the earliest disciples, we, too, filled with His Spirit, are called to be His witnesses—to do the works of Jesus. The conditions are believing and asking in His name. We have been given Resurrection-based authority to act on His behalf. Be encouraged to believe it. Let's ask in His name that He would grant us His Holy Spirit that we might do the greater works!

KEYS OF THE KINGDOM
(Matt. 16:18, 19)

After Peter made his great confession of his faith in the messiahship of Jesus as God's Son, Jesus made a stunning revelation to him. Turn to Matthew 16:18, 19.

◇ Who did Peter say Jesus was? (v. 16)

_____

_____

◇ Who builds the church, and whose church is it? (v. 18)

_____

_____

◇ What will not be able to stand against this church? (v. 18)

_____

_____

◇ To whom are the "keys of the kingdom of heaven" given? For what purpose? (v. 19)

_____

_____

Jesus said He would build His church. Not even "the gates of Hades" would stand against it. This expression means that the power of death cannot prevent the advance of the kingdom, nor claim victory over those who belong to God. It is a reference to

Jesus' Resurrection which, achieved through His Cross, is the foundation of the church. Thus, the apostle Paul declared, "No other foundation can anyone lay than that which is laid, which is Jesus Christ" (1 Cor. 3:11).

KINGDOM EXTRA

God-given authority—greater works—the keys of the kingdom—binding and loosing—"on this rock I will build My church"—these truths are staggering in their implications. But how the church is to apply these truths has been a matter of diverse opinion and is worthy of further study. A student may wish to gain further insight by consulting the *New Spirit-Filled Life Bible* by Thomas Nelson Publishers, 2002 (annotated notes, Matt. 16:18, 19, p. 1320; annotated notes, John 14:12, p. 1469; Kingdom Dynamic, John 14:12, 13: "Expect Greater Things," p. 1469).

Kingdom ministry is Jesus' ministry. He has transmitted it to us in His name and by His authority, granting us the keys of the kingdom of heaven. Jesus is the Messiah whose words and works fulfilled His Father's will to redeem a sinful and fallen world. He was anointed by the Spirit of God to proclaim the kingdom of God. And by this same Spirit He anoints us as His disciples to be His witnesses.

"Greater works" are now possible because Jesus has returned to the Father and sent His Spirit. Kingdom ministry not only continues, it expands. But kingdom ministry requires kingdom power. This is the topic of our next lesson.

FAITH ALIVE

To our finite minds, it seems presumptuous to expect to do greater works than Jesus does. Certainly, He is God, and we are frail humans! Knowing that, how can you integrate His promise of greater works into your experience with humility, yet faith?

POWER OF THE KINGDOM
Lesson 4

THE BIG IDEA

A promise isn't a "maybe" or a "hope so" in the Bible. It is a sure thing. Let's investigate the promise and reality of Holy Spirit power demonstrated by Jesus and anticipated by the prophets.

THE PROMISE OF THE FATHER
(Acts 1:3–8; Luke 24:48, 49)

After His Resurrection, Jesus had just forty days to mentor His disciples. He had been to the Cross, and now it was time for Him to focus on what His disciples needed in order to be effective witnesses. Telling them not to leave Jerusalem until the "Promise of the Father" had been fulfilled, He spoke of the coming of the Holy Spirit who would empower them for ministry (Acts 1:4; Luke 24:49).

Let's start by looking at the Word Wealth definition of "promise." Read it to see how sure the promises of God really are!

WORD WEALTH

Promise, *epangelia* (Acts 13:32). Both a promise and the thing promised, an announcement with the special sense of promise, pledge, and offer. *Epangelia* tells what the promise from God is and then gives the assurance that the thing promised will be done.

FAITH ALIVE

◇ What is the difference between an earthly promise ("I hope so") and God's promise ("the Promise of the Father")?

_____

_____

◈ What confidence does it give you that the Lord carries His promises to completion?

_____

_____

Now, let's look closely at the "Promise of the Father" mentioned by Jesus in the Books of Acts and Luke.

◈ Turn to Acts 1:3–5. What two teachings did Jesus focus on between His Resurrection and Ascension?

_____

_____

What were the disciples to wait for? (v. 4)

_____

_____

What will they be baptized with? (v. 5)

_____

_____

How soon was the Spirit's coming to be? (v. 5)

_____

_____

What will the disciples be empowered to do? (v. 8)

_____

_____

◈ Turn to Luke 24:46–49. Who will be sending the "Promise of My Father?" (v. 49)

_____

_____

◈ What will the "Promise of My Father" enable the church to do? (Luke 24:47–49)

_____

_____

◇ In Luke 3:16, John the Baptist had promised that "One mightier than I" is coming to "baptize you with the Holy Spirit and fire." Who is that One?

_____

_____

_____

THE PROMISED HELPER
(John 14:16)

Jesus called the Holy Spirit a "Helper." What do these verses say about the promised Helper?

John 14:16, 17 _____

_____

_____

John 14:26 _____

_____

_____

John 15:26 _____

_____

_____

John 16:7, 8 _____

_____

_____

Not only would the Helper bear witness concerning Jesus to His disciples, He would also bear witness through them to the world.

Note that Jesus used the terminology "another Helper" in John 14:16. Let's mine the Word Wealth riches of both of those words.

WORD WEALTH

Another, *allos* (John 14:16). One besides, another of the same kind. The word shows similarities but diversities of operation and ministries. Jesus' use of *allos* for sending another Comforter equals "one besides Me and in addition to Me but one just like Me.

He will do in My absence what I would do if I were physically present with you." The Spirit's coming assures continuity with what Jesus did and taught.

Helper, *parakletos* (John 15:26). From *para*, "beside," and *kaleo*, "to call," hence, called to one's side. The word signifies an intercessor, comforter, helper, advocate, counselor. In nonbiblical literature, *parakletos* had the technical meaning of an attorney who appears in court on another's behalf. The Holy Spirit leads believers to a greater apprehension of gospel truths. In addition to general help and guidance, He gives the strength to endure the hostility of the world system.

◇ What is the significance of Jesus' use of "another" Helper?

_____

_____

_____

◇ What does the Helper do?

_____

_____

_____

THE SPIRIT IN THE OLD TESTAMENT

Anticipation of the Spirit's coming reaches far back into Old Testament history, many years before John the Baptist and Jesus spoke of it. From time to time, the Spirit would come upon leaders, giving them wisdom and prophetic anointing as they led God's people. We see also prophetic references to the Spirit's coming. To fill in the background of the promise of the Holy Spirit through the entire body of Scripture, let's study several Old Testament examples.

◇ Read Numbers 11:24–29. What was Moses' wish? (v. 29)

_____

_____

_____

_____

_____

◇ What happened to David when Samuel anointed him with oil? (1 Sam. 16:13)

_____

_____

_____

◇ Turn to Joel 2:28, 29. This is one of the texts used in Peter's Pentecost message (Acts 2:17, 18). It awakens God's people to His purpose of reaching the world through all who would be available to the work of His Spirit. What was Joel's prophetic promise?

_____

_____

_____

Should you desire further study, check out Judges 14:19; 1 Samuel 10:10, 11; 1 Samuel 19:19–21; 1 Chronicles 15:1, 2; 2 Chronicles 24:20; Ezekiel 11:5.

There was coming a day when the promise of the Spirit would be for all God's people. Jesus said that the Holy Spirit will remain forever and will dwell with you and in you (John 14:16, 17). What an amazing promise—a universal, eternal, and internal coming of the Spirit! But also, what an essential promise! Without its fulfillment God's people would be powerless.

RECEIVING THE PROMISE
(Acts 2:1–21)

Let's move to the New Testament, to the place where the Father's promise of the Spirit was about to be fulfilled. In the second chapter of Acts, about 120 people had obeyed Jesus' instructions to wait in Jerusalem until they were endued with power from on high. Something that would transform everyone was about to take place.

◇ Before answering any questions, read Acts 2:1–21 in its entirety.

_____

_____

_____

◈ What is the significance of the people being in "one accord" in verse 1?

◈ Describe what happened in verses 2–4.

◈ What is suggested to your mind by the signs of windlike sound and firelike tongues? (vv. 2, 3) You may want to consult Matthew 3:11; Exodus 3:2; 19:16–19; 1 Kings 19:11, 12.

◈ What evidence do you see that the filling with the Holy Spirit was meant for all who sought it, and not just for a few religious leaders? (Note the words "all," "whole," "each" in Acts 2:1–4; Joel 2:28, 29.)

◈ According to Acts 2:4, what was the immediate result of the Spirit's filling? (Note what they were speaking in verse 11.)

◈ Because the languages spoken represented up to 15 different areas of the Roman Empire, many who heard the 120 speaking recognized their "mother tongue." However, some mockers didn't recognize any languages and thought that these people were drunken (v. 13). How did Peter answer them? (v. 15, 16)

◈ What Old Testament promise did Peter recite? (vv. 16–21)

Jesus had told His followers to wait in Jerusalem and expect power (Luke 24:49). There was no hint given about what would happen, but clearly the evidence shows that Jesus knew what would occur and would make it abundantly clear to them. "The Promise of My Father" and all they experienced at the coming of the Holy Spirit on Pentecost are one and the same.

As the Baptizer with the Holy Spirit (Luke 3:16), Jesus' instruction to His followers in Luke 11:13 to "ask" for the Holy Spirit and to wait until they receive power is pertinent to all believers for all times. All who believe are to ask and expect God to fill them with His Spirit and to be empowered for their mission to serve Him. It is this supernatural *power* that Jesus uses to fulfill His mission to the world through His church.

THE HOLY SPIRIT POINTS PEOPLE TO JESUS
(Acts 2:14–47)

Peter's first recorded act after being filled with the Holy Spirit was to preach Jesus. As a result, the Holy Spirit convicted many people of their sin of rejecting their Messiah. Peter's entire sermon is recorded in Acts 2:14–36.

◈ Acts 2:37 says Peter's message so powerfully impacted the people that they were "cut to the heart." What do you think this means?

_____

_____

◈ What did the people ask? (v. 37)

_____

_____

◈ In response, what two things did Peter tell them to do? (v. 38)

_____

_____

◈ How many people were saved that day? (v. 41)

_____

_____

THE HOLY SPIRIT AND NEW BIRTH
(John 20:19–23)

Many people wonder what the difference is between the Holy Spirit's filling and anointing with power for witness (Acts 1:5; 2:4) and the Holy Spirit's role in the new birth experience (John 3:3; 20:22). Let's turn to John 20:19–23 where Jesus appeared to His disciples after He was raised from the dead, but before the promised coming of the Holy Spirit at Pentecost.

◈ What did Jesus say and do in John 20:22?

_____

_____

_____

_____

_____

Jesus' words here, "Receive the Holy Spirit," help to set in context two different works of the Holy Spirit in the believer's life:

(1) On Easter night, the disciples do, in fact, "receive the Holy Spirit" as "the Spirit of life" (Rom. 8:2). Jesus' Word is direct and unequivocal: "Receive"; and in doing so, the disciples are "born again" (John 3:3) by the Holy Spirit's regenerating work in them (Rom. 8:11–17). This passage parallels the breath of the Father on Adam in the first creation, as Jesus breathes on them and the "new creation" is begun (2 Cor. 5:17).

(2) However, on Pentecost the work of God's Spirit as the Spirit of power (Is. 11:2, "might") is to enable Jesus' disciples for ministry—witness and service—to fulfill their mission to the world.

BE FILLED WITH THE SPIRIT
(Acts 4:8, 23–31; Eph. 5:18)

In the Book of Acts, people filled with the Holy Spirit were also refilled subsequently. For example, when Peter spoke to the Jewish religious leaders in defense of the faith, Scripture says that he was "filled with the Holy Spirit" (Acts 4:8). These same words were used to indicate Peter's initial experience of being "filled with the Holy Spirit" (Acts 2:4). We will see from this and other examples in Scripture that a believer's interaction with the Spirit is never static; it is a dynamic ongoing relationship of the Spirit's power and anointing.

◈ Compare Acts 2:4 and Acts 4:8. Why do you think the same term "filled with the Holy Spirit" is used in both scriptures?

_____

_____

◈ Turn to Acts 4:23–31 and read the account of a filling of an entire group of believers after the Day of Pentecost. Why did they need to be "filled" again? (vv. 23–28)

_____

_____

◈ What was their request? (Acts 4:29, 30)

_____

_____

◈ How did the Lord answer their request? (Acts 4:31)

_____

_____

_____

Spirit fullness is not merely a state, but a repeated experience of the Holy Spirit's anointing or filling. Note that Paul, after his initial filling with the Spirit (Acts 9:17), also was refilled with the Holy Spirit (Acts 13:9) as he faced a difficult circumstance.

◈ Compare Acts 9:17 and Acts 13:9. Then look at what was happening in each situation. What role did the Holy Spirit have in both circumstances? (Acts 9:1–18; 13:4–12)

_____

_____

_____

Ephesians 5:18 says that the will of the Lord is that we "be filled with the Spirit." It is interesting to note that the tense of the Greek verb for "be filled" in this verse indicates that such a Spirit-filled condition does not stop with a single experience, but is maintained by continually being filled by the Spirit. It is important to realize that the initial immersion or infilling of the Holy Spirit is a *gate*, not a *goal*. It is the beginning, not the end, of Spirit fullness!

FAITH ALIVE

Turn to Ephesians 5:18. What does this verse say to you?

THE PROMISE IS FOR YOU
(Acts 2:39)

The kingdom of God is to be released through us by the power of God given to us. The promise of the Spirit's presence in power is given, therefore, to every child of God. From earliest times the hope had been that the Spirit would be outpoured on all flesh. At Pentecost this hope was realized and made available to every person God called to salvation.

◈ Turn again to Peter's first sermon on the Day of Pentecost in the second chapter of Acts. To whom is the promise given? Could that include you? (Acts 2:39)

_____

_____

◈ Read Luke 11:9–13. What does the Father promise to give to those who ask Him? (v. 13)

_____

_____

FAITH ALIVE

_____

◈ How does Jesus' promise of bestowing Holy Spirit power to the church affect you today?

_____

_____

◈ If you would you like to be filled with the Holy Spirit, simply ask.

_____

_____

KINGDOM EXTRA

The Holy Spirit and His relationship to the believer and the church, past and present, are subjects worthy of comprehensive study. For your further study, may we recommend the *New Spirit-Filled Life Bible*, (Thomas Nelson, 2002):

1. Kingdom Dynamics: all "HOLY SPIRIT FULLNESS" articles beginning with "Victory in the Fullness of the Holy Spirit," Psalm 110:1, page 774;
2. Bible Introductions: all "The Holy Spirit at Work" sections, especially for Acts, pages 1486–87;
3. Annotated notes: Acts 1:5—2:39, pages 1489–94;
4. Truth in Action: Acts, pages 1544–45;
5. Article: "Holy Spirit Gifts and Power," pages 1849–58;
6. Article: "The Holy Spirit and Restoration," pages 1859–64.

PRAYER AND THE KINGDOM
Lesson 5

THE BIG IDEA

Prayer offered to God in the power of the Spirit makes a difference! Invite God's kingdom rule as you pray, "Your kingdom come."

YOUR KINGDOM COME!
(Matt. 6:9–13)

There was something so compelling about the way Jesus prayed that caused one of His disciples to say, "Lord, teach us to pray." Not only did He demonstrate how to pray by His example of close communion with the Father, He said a prayer that has become known to millions as "The Lord's Prayer."

Jesus gave this prayer to His disciples not as a formula for repetition, but as an outline for dynamic expansion of the kingdom by people who have truly committed themselves to the King. The prayer appears in Matthew 6:9–13 (Luke 11:2–4 is a shortened form). Read the prayer in both places before answering the questions from Matthew's account.

◈ What is the difference between Jesus' prayer and the kind of "phony" prayers He describes in Matthew 6:5–8?

_____

_____

Let's take a look at the Word Wealth meaning of the word "pray" used in verse 6.

WORD WEALTH

Pray, *proseuchomai* (Matt. 6:6). The word is progressive. Starting with the noun, *euche*, which is a prayer to God that also includes making a vow, the word expands to the verb *euchomai*, a special term describing an invocation, request, or entreaty. Adding *pros,* "in the direction of" (God), *proseuchomai* becomes the most frequent word for prayer.

◇ Does this Word Wealth definition indicate that a person's participation in prayer is active or passive? What leads you to say that?

_____

_____

Now, let's study the Lord's Prayer beginning at Matthew 6:9. Note that the prayer is divided into two major parts. The first part addresses God's concerns; the second part addresses ours.

◇ What is the significance of the words "our Father"? (v. 9)

_____

◇ What are the first three requests? (vv. 9, 10)

_____

_____

_____

◇ What are the next three requests? (vv. 11–13)

_____

_____

_____

◇ Whose concerns are voiced in verses 11–13? verses 9, 10?

_____

_____

◇ How does the promise of God's provision, pardon, and protection offered in this prayer comfort you?

_____

_____

_____

◇ Now look at Matthew 6:8 to see what Jesus said just before giving the prayer. As we give priority to His concerns, what does this verse say about God's readiness to meet our needs?

_____

The "Lord's Prayer" helps us understand the nature of prayer. It is an invitation to ask and receive daily from our heavenly Father physical provision, forgiveness, and spiritual protection. He knows what we need even before we ask. But it is in the larger context of God's honor, kingdom, and will that the receiving of such personal answers take on their true significance. He invites us to partner with His desires as we seek the answers to our own. As He has made meeting our daily needs His priority, He asks that we make seeking His kingdom and righteousness our priority! In so doing we make possible not only the fulfilling of our personal needs, but the accomplishing of His redemptive purposes.

Thus, in anticipation of the final consummation of God's kingdom and His saving purposes, we ask that His name be honored today in this world. As His children, we request that this happen by His kingdom coming and His will being done on earth as it is in heaven.

FAITH ALIVE

Genuine prayer is not an attempt to get God to meet our desires and demands; rather, as we pray and subordinate our will to His, the doorway is opened to His fullest blessings being released in our lives. Ask the Lord to help you implement the Lord's Prayer into your prayer life so that His blessing is released in you and through you.

PERSISTENTLY RESISTING THE STATUS QUO
(Luke 18:1–8)

As we patiently long for the full manifestation of God's righteous rule on earth at the end of this age, we faithfully persist in resisting the "status quo" in this age. This helps guard us against discouragement. Through prayer we insist that what "is" must come under the "ought" of God's kingdom—today! Jesus Himself taught us to do so!

In the parable of the persistent widow in Luke 18:1–8, we learn a valuable lesson about the persistence of prayer.

◇ What are the main facts of the story?

_____

_____

_____

◇ Sometimes this parable is misunderstood. Jesus is not comparing God to the judge in terms of His unwillingness to hear our requests. Rather, this parable is using contrast rather than comparison as a teaching tool. Knowing that, what truth about God's kingdom does this parable teach?

_____

_____

_____

◇ In what way do you think the truth of this parable differs from common perceptions or misconceptions?

_____

_____

_____

KINGDOM EXTRA

This parable encourages us that God will avenge those who cry out to Him. It is important to understand that *avenge* is not *revenge*; it has to do with justice. It encourages us that the Father, who is the Just Judge, will bring us redress from wrong when we pray. Let's take an in-depth look at the word.

"Avenge" comes from the Greek *ekdikeo* (*ek*, "out," and *dike*, "justice") meaning that which proceeds from justice. It has to do with vindicating a person's right or righting a wrong. The verb *ekdikeo* appears six times in the New Testament and is used regarding the vindication of the rights of a widow (Luke 18: 3, 5) and God's avenging of the blood of the martyrs (Rev. 6:10; 19:2). The noun *ekdikos* is used twice, regarding civil authorities who exact a penalty from a wrongdoer (Rom. 13:4) and of the Lord who does likewise with one who wrongs his brother, especially in the matter of adultery (1 Thess. 4:6). The noun *ekdikesis*, "vengeance," is found nine times and is used in three passages with the verb *poieo*, "to make," and thus means "avenge" (Luke 18:7, 8; Acts 7:24). Twice *ekdikesis* is used in a statement that "vengeance" belongs to the Lord (Rom. 12:19; Heb. 10:30). In 2 Thessalonians 1:8, it is God who rightly exacts justice, without vindictiveness, upon those "who do not know God, and ... do not obey the gospel of our Lord Jesus Christ."

The parable of the persistent widow underscores God's willingness to hear the prayers of His chosen ones who persistently cry out to Him to right life's wrongs and see the righteous rule of God replace the rule of evil men. It is a passionate cry to see "His kingdom come and His will be done on earth as it is in heaven."

FAITH ALIVE

Why do we give up so quickly? Why do we faint in prayer so readily? Is it because we believe it won't make a difference? Thus we accept, perhaps unwillingly, the situation as unchangeable. The poor widow could not stop insisting on justice, because she believed it would make a difference—and it did! She prayed until the situation changed.

How much more will such continuance with God bring results! He is no wicked judge. He is the One who has invited us as His chosen ones to ask His kingdom to come and His will to be done. Have you wearied of praying? The parable is for you. You will reap in due season if you faint not.

◇ What steps can you take to build confidence that your prayers do make a difference? Begin to apply those things to the situations and people for whom you are praying.

HOUSE OF PRAYER FOR ALL NATIONS
(Mark 11:15–18; 1 Tim. 2:1–6)

The nature and power of prayer in petitioning our heavenly Father to accomplish His will and purpose on earth is indeed an awesome and amazing reality. It is an awesome reality because God invites us to partner in the fulfillment of His redemptive purposes on earth. It is an amazing reality because it works! Oh, the unfathomable wisdom and mercy of our Sovereign Creator and Redeeming Savior! Although there is a God-ordained limit as to the full coming of His kingdom on earth now, there is no such limit as to whom God wants to receive the initial blessings of His kingdom before this age ends. He wants people of all nations to experience the benefits of His transforming rule through the Good News of the gospel of Jesus Christ.

Jesus' reflection of the Father's compassion for all nations is seen in His response to the merchandising of the moneychangers in the temple courts in Mark 11:15–18.

◇ What did Jesus do in verses 15–17?

_____

_____

◇ What is the significance of the two statements Jesus made in verse 17? Look up the Old Testament context for each.

1. "My house shall be called a house of prayer for all nations" (compare with Is. 56:7).

_____

_____

2. "You have made it a den of thieves" (compare with Jer. 7:11).

_____

_____

_____

◇ To dig deeper, look what happened before and after Jesus cleansed the temple (Mark 11:12–14; 20–24). When He saw an unfruitful fig tree, what did Jesus do in verse 14?

_____

_____

_____

◇ What was the immediate result? (v. 20, 21)

_____

_____

What did this all mean? The withered tree had become a symbol of national Israel's lack of the fruit of repentance. The universal witness of God through His ancient people, Israel, was coming to an end. His original intention was that His dwelling place would be the place where the prayers of people from all nations would be heard and answered—that "all peoples of the earth may know Your name and fear You" (2 Chr. 6:33). Instead it had been corrupted.

◇ What do you think were Jesus' heart and attitude as He cleansed the temple and cursed the fig tree?

_____

_____

_____

◇ How did cleansing the temple pave the way for the reestablishment of God's purpose that His temple would be a house of prayer for all nations?

_____

_____

◇ Who is the temple now? (Eph. 2:19–22)

_____

_____

The literal temple building in Jerusalem would be destroyed in A.D. 70. Still, God's gracious intention of prayer being offered for all nations remained intact.

Turn to 1 Timothy 2:1–6 to see what the apostle Paul said about the place of prayer among God's people.

◇ For whom are we to pray with thanksgiving? (1 Tim. 2:1, 2)

_____

_____

◇ Why are we to pray like this for such people? What are the results? (v. 2)

_____

_____

◇ Why are such results "good and acceptable in the sight of God"? What is His desire? (vv. 3, 4)

_____

_____

Prayer and resisting the status quo are connected with world evangelization. What do these verses teach about prayer and God's purpose for the spread of the gospel?

Ephesians 6:18, 19

_____

_____

Colossians 4:2–4

_____

_____

2 Peter 3:9

_____

_____

Our intercession for all nations is to be a reflection of God's desire that none perish. Therefore, our gathering places should be characterized by *prayer* for all nations and the *presence* of all nations as God opens the door of salvation to them in answer to our faithful and compassionate petitions.

AWESOME RELATIONSHIP, AWESOME CALL
(Rom. 8:18–26)

Romans 8:26 offers a wonderful truth to those who have received the privilege to be called the children of God.

◈ Who helps us pray? How is this described in verse 26?

_____

_____

◈ Look at two other places in this text where "groaning" is mentioned. What are they? (vv. 22, 23)

_____

_____

It is important to see that because the promised kingdom of righteousness has come in Jesus Christ, there is now a "groaning" and a yearning as we await the full revelation of God's rule in the age to come. In the meantime, we are to pray with confidence that the Holy Spirit is leading and helping us pray with "groanings which cannot be uttered."

As we do pray, these truths will guide us:

1. Prayer sees things as they are, while worship sees things as they should be—God rightfully honored as Sovereign Creator and Redeeming Savior!

2. Prayer sees that man wrongfully usurped God's rule, violated His law, and destroyed His creation.

3. Believing prayer insists this must change!

4. Thus, prayer becomes an expression of the deep-seated desire and groaning to see wrongs righted, sin abolished, death destroyed, and the curse removed—to see *God's kingdom come and His will be done on earth as it is in heaven.*

FAITH ALIVE

We have studied prayer—now let's get to it! As you spend time in prayer this week, incorporate what we have studied here.

WORSHIP IN THE KINGDOM
Lesson 6

THE BIG IDEA

Prayer invites God's rule, worship releases His reign. Discover how you can welcome the King through your worship.

WHAT IS WORSHIP?

Worship is at the heart of Spirit-filled living. When the Holy Spirit was poured out on the Day of Pentecost, what was the immediate consequence? It was to praise God for His "wonderful works" of redemption through His Son, Jesus Christ (Acts 2:11). Such praise prepared the way for God's saving rule to be proclaimed and experienced in the lives of 3,000 people who put their full trust in the crucified Christ as the reigning Messiah and Lord.

In order to deepen our experience of worship, let's focus on its meaning.

WORD WEALTH

Worship, *proskuneo* (Rev. 4:10). From *pros*, "toward," and *kuneo*, "to kiss." To prostrate oneself, bow down, do obeisance, show reverence, do homage, worship, adore. In the New Testament, the word especially denotes homage rendered to God and the ascended Christ. All believers have a one-dimensional worship, to the only Lord and Savior. We do not worship angels, saints, shrines, relics, or religious personages.

◊ What is the difference between worship of the living God and worship of things or other people?

_____

_____

◊ How can a person be assured that his worship is vital and real?

WORSHIP IN SPIRIT AND TRUTH
(John 4:23, 24)

Jesus teaches clearly about the nature of worship to a woman who met her Messiah at a well! Here, Jesus turned her evasive question about where to worship into an opportunity to teach her about true worship. Out of this conversation came one of the most profound truths of the nature of worship—that worship is not mere form and ceremony, but spiritual reality, which is in harmony with the nature of God, who is Spirit.

◈ Write out what Jesus said about worship in John 4:24.

_____

_____

_____

◈ What is more important—where we worship or whom we worship? (John 4:21, 22)

_____

_____

◈ What is God the Father seeking? Why? (John 4:23, 24)

_____

_____

This passage teaches that it is our responsibility to learn how the Lord wants to be worshiped. It is essential that we cultivate a relationship with Him out of which sincere, Holy Spirit-enabled worship will flow.

1. We are to worship God "in spirit." We are alive through new birth and aglow with Holy Spirit enablement (John 1:12, 13; 3:6, 7; 1 Cor. 14:15). Worship is not mechanical, rote, or merely human activity but dynamically capacitated spiritual action.

2. We worship Him "in truth." Worship done in truth is sincere, transparent, and according to biblical mandates. The word translated "truth" in this passage is the Greek word <u>alethia</u>. Let's look at the meaning of this great word.

WORD WEALTH

Truth, *alethia* (John 4:24). Derived from negative, *a*, and *lanthano*, "to be hidden," "to escape notice." (Compare "latent," "lethargy," "lethal.") *Aletheia* is the opposite of fictitious, feigned, or false. It denotes veracity, reality, sincerity, accuracy, integrity, truthfulness, dependability, and propriety.

◇ From what we have just studied, put in your own words what it means to worship the Lord in truth.

_____

_____

_____

◇ What does it mean to worship the Lord in spirit?

_____

_____

_____

FAITH ALIVE

Does it strike you that God is *seeking* to find someone who worships Him in spirit and truth? Write what heart attitude or understanding you can work on this week that will deepen your worship of the Lord.

SACRIFICE OF PRAISE
(Heb. 13:15)

The writer of Hebrews encourages us to "continually offer the sacrifice of praise to God, that is the fruit of our lips, giving thanks to His name" (Heb. 13:15).

Why is praising God a sacrifice? The word "sacrifice" (Greek *thusia*) comes from the root *thuo*, a verb meaning "to kill or slaughter for a purpose." Praise often requires that we "kill" our pride, fear, or sloth—anything that threatens to diminish or interfere with our worship of the Lord. We also discover here the basis of all our praise: the sacrifice of our Lord Jesus Christ. It is by Him, in Him, with Him, to Him, and for Him that we offer our sacrifice of praise to God.

Praise will never be successfully hindered when we keep its focus on Him—the Founder and Completer of our salvation. His Cross, His blood—His love gift of life and forgiveness to us—keep praise as a living sacrifice!

FAITH ALIVE

David said he would not offer to the Lord that which cost him nothing (2 Sam. 24:24). How can you integrate the truth of the sacrifice of praise into your worship experience?

GOD IS ENTHRONED IN PRAISE
(Ps. 22:3)

Few principles are more essential to our understanding than this one: *the presence of God's kingdom power is directly related to the practice of God's praise.* God is "enthroned in the praises" of His people, says Psalm 22:3. The verb "enthroned" indicates that wherever God's people exalt His name, He is ready to manifest His kingdom's power in the way most appropriate to the situation, as His rule is invited to invade our setting.

It is this fact that properly leads many to conclude that in a very real way, praise prepares a specific and present place for God among His people. Some have chosen the term "establish His throne" to describe this "enthroning" of God in our midst by our worshiping and praising welcome. God awaits the prayerful and praise-filled worship of His people as an entry point for His kingdom to "come"—to enter, that His "will be done" in human circumstances. (See Luke 11:2–4 and Ps. 93:2.) We do not manipulate God, but align ourselves with the great kingdom truth: His is the power, ours is the privilege (and responsibility) to welcome Him into our world—our private, present world or the circumstances of our society.

◇ Look up Psalm 22:3. What characteristic of God is connected with praise?

_____

_____

◇ What does the verb "enthroned" indicate?

_____

_____

◇ What is the difference between welcoming God into our situation through praise and manipulating Him to get what we want?

A millennium later, Jesus quoted from this psalm from the Cross in His cry, "My God, My God, why have You forsaken me?" (Mark 15:34; Matt. 27:46). Feeling the apparent abandonment of the Father, His call was not in vain. God heard and answered, and dramatically and decisively delivered Him from death three days later. Alive forevermore, Jesus Christ now stands as the greatest and grandest example of the faithfulness of God in delivering those who rightly honor Him in total trust. Truly, God is the Holy One who inhabits the praise and cries of His own. Worship recognizes that this is God's essential nature and enthrones Him on the praises of His people. And in so doing, He is welcomed to increasingly further His saving and delivering work.

KINGDOM EXTRA

"Enthroned on the praises of Israel"—this phrase translates a Hebrew phrase which literally means "sitting on the praises of Israel." It is the picture of a king sitting on his throne in ruling splendor. In this case the king is God Himself and the throne is the praise of His people, Israel. The combination of words suggests dwelling and tarrying. In the picturesque words of Franz Delitzsch: "The songs of praise, which resounded in Israel as the memorials of His deeds of deliverance, are like the wings of the cherubim, upon which His presence hovered in Israel" (*Keil & Delitzsch Commentary on the Old Testament: Psalms*, p. 303). Thus, the phrase also could be translated "God is the praise of Israel" in line with Deuteronomy 10:21 where Moses says, "He is your praise, and He is your God, who has done for you these great and awesome things which your eyes have seen." Either way, the message is clear. God is King and is to be rightly honored as such, for He has faithfully and consistently delivered His people. To so worship and extol Him properly enthrones Him and acknowledges and allows His right to rule as Savior and Deliverer of His people.

PRAISE AND THE PRESENCE OF GOD
(2 Chr. 20:1–30)

Whenever and wherever God's people praise Him, He reigns among them and does miraculous things on their behalf. Perhaps the most well-known Old Testament story illustrating this truth is the story of how God delivered Judah and King Jehoshaphat from annihilation by their enemies.

Turn to 2 Chronicles 20:1–30.

◇ Faced with overwhelming odds, what did the king call the people to do? (vv. 3, 4)

_____

_____

_____

◇ What did Jehoshaphat pray? (vv. 6–12)

_____

_____

_____

◇ What did the Lord say in response to the prayer? (vv. 15–17)

_____

_____

◇ The day of the battle, what unusual "battle tactic" did the people use? (vv. 21, 22)

_____

_____

◇ What happened as they moved forward in battle? (vv. 22–27)

_____

_____

◇ What was the long-term result of this event? (vv. 28–30)

_____

_____

These verses highlight the final key in Judah's miraculous deliverance. As they began to sing and to praise God with the expectancy that He would fight for them, their enemies were defeated. Although such dramatic deliverance by placing praisers before the warriors is unusual in military action, the basic principle of rightly honoring the Lord as the only true sovereign over His people is what accounts for the victories of Israel over their enemies throughout the Old Testament.

◈ For extra study: Scan other Old Testament victories in Joshua 6:10, 20; Judges 2—16; 1 Samuel 11, 17, 28—31; 2 Samuel 7—10. What general features do these examples have in common?

UNIVERSAL WORSHIP: GOD IS KING
(Ps. 145)

"The LORD has established His throne in heaven, and His kingdom rules over all" (Ps. 103:19). Worship has to do with rulership. Kings are honored for their authority to rule. But God alone is King over all the earth. He alone is the ultimate Ruler from whom all earthly kings derive their ruling authority (Rom. 13:1). He alone "puts down one, and exalts another" (Ps. 75:7). Therefore, universal worship is due His name. He alone is King of kings, and His rule is a benevolent rule—"The LORD is good to all" (Ps. 145:9).

Turn to Psalm 145.

◈ How did David respond to the reality that God's rule is good? (v. 10)

◈ What do the saints speak of in their blessing of God? (v. 11)

◈ What is the result of such blessing of God? (v. 12)

◈ What is the nature of God's kingdom? (v. 13)

◈ The Lord is near to what kind of person? (v. 18)

REASONS TO PRAISE GOD

The psalmist says that all people are called to clap and shout praise to God because "He is a great King over all the earth" (Ps. 47:1, 2). They are to "sing praises with understanding" (v. 7).

◈ Look at Psalm 47:8, 9 and discover what such "understanding" includes. Write down the reasons the psalmist gave for praising God as King of all the earth.

◈ In the New Testament, what does Paul say needs to happen in the believer? (Eph. 1:18)

◈ The reasons to praise God are many! Listed are just a few. Look up these verses and give the reason why they say to praise Him.

1 Chronicles 16:23–29

---

1 Chronicles 29:11–14

Psalm 103:19–22

Colossians 1:13, 14

Colossians 1:18

To know God in truth is to worship Him truly. We will sing praises with understanding, too, when we see what the people who praised God in Scripture saw. Our understanding of God is the foundation of our worship of God and allows His right to rule as Savior and Deliverer of His people.

FAITH ALIVE

◇ Using your Bible, write down at least seven reasons to praise God. You can use the Scriptures used in this study or find your own.

1. _____

2. _____

3. _____

4. _____

5. _____

6. _____

7. _____

◇ What things has God worked in your life that you have reason to praise Him for? List seven. Take one reason per day and praise God for that as you worship Him.

1. _____

2. _____

3. _____

4. _____

5. _____

6. _____

7. _____

◇ Taking the essence of this prayer, worship the Lord: "Father, help me see that true worship enthrones You, the God Who is Spirit and Truth. Rule in righteousness in my life as I worship You in spirit and truth. I thank You that You seek a worshiper such as this. O Father, assist me by Your Spirit to worship You in truth as Jesus taught so I will reflect the glory of Your salvation to our world."

_____

_____

_____

CHARACTER AND THE KINGDOM

Lesson 7

THE BIG IDEA

Not only do you enter the kingdom, the kingdom enters you!

WHO DO WE LOOK LIKE?

No kingdom is more significant than God's kingdom. As citizens of God's kingdom, we who are disciples of Jesus Christ are to reflect the character of the One in whose kingdom we live. The character of the King and His kingdom becomes our character. When that happens, we will live differently because we have been profoundly transformed. We are in God, and He is in us (1 John 4:15).

◇ When we have truly repented of self-focused living and have fully believed the Good News of Jesus Christ, who will we live for? (2 Cor. 5:15)

_____

_____

◇ What does 2 Corinthians 5:17 say about our life in Christ?

_____

_____

◇ Whose kingdom have we been delivered from, and in whose kingdom are we now? (Col. 1:13)

_____

_____

◇ Who has qualified us to be partakers of the inheritance? (Col. 1:12)

_____

_____

◇ Read 2 Peter 1:2–4. What will we be "partakers of"? What does that mean?

_____

_____

◇ According to Romans 14:17, the kingdom of God consists of what three things? Does that encourage you to press on in your discipleship?

_____

_____

Scripture says that the evidence of His life reflected in us is being "filled with the fruits of righteousness which are by Jesus Christ, to the glory and praise of God" (Phil. 1:11). We will now study the characteristics of those who are becoming "partakers" as sons and daughters of the King.

RIGHTEOUSNESS IN THE KINGDOM
(Matt. 5:21–48)

What do you think of when you hear the word "righteousness"? For many of us, images come to mind which are based on unflattering stereotypes of self-righteous people. Let's discover how righteousness is used in Scripture.

WORD WEALTH

Righteousness, _dikaiosune_ (2 Tim. 4:8). Just, the quality of being right. Broadly, the word suggests conformity to the revealed will of God in all respects. _Dikaiosune_ is both judicial and gracious. God declares the believer righteous, in the sense of acquitting him, and imparts righteousness to him.

◇ Look up 2 Corinthians 5:21. On what grounds can we claim righteousness?

_____

_____

Although our righteousness before God is through Christ's work alone, and while we cannot earn any spiritual gift or right to function in the power of the Holy Spirit, integrity and morality of character are nonetheless essential to the "kingdom person." Holiness of heart and life keeps open the lines of communication with God by keeping any private or carnal agenda out of the way.

◇ Turn to Galatians 5:19–25. What is the difference between the works of the flesh and the fruit of the Spirit?

_____

_____

Jesus gave an apt description of God's standard of righteousness that characterizes the citizens of His kingdom. His righteousness stood in stark contrast to the self-centered "religious" righteousness of the scribes and Pharisees, which was artificial, external, legalistic, and burdensome. Let's look at how Jesus compared such "righteousness" with the true righteousness of God's kingdom. Write down the six contrasts He gives in Matthew 5:

	"RELIGIOUS" RIGHTEOUSNESS Keeps the letter of the Law	KINGDOM RIGHTEOUSNESS Fulfills the spirit of the Law
Matthew 5:21–26		
Matthew 5:27–30		
Matthew 5:31, 32		
Matthew 5:33–37		

	"RELIGIOUS" RIGHTEOUSNESS Keeps the letter of the Law	KINGDOM RIGHTEOUSNESS Fulfills the spirit of the Law
Matthew 5:38–42		
Matthew 5:43–48		

◈ Based on what we have just studied, what is the main difference between "religious" righteousness and *kingdom* righteousness?

_____

_____

Kingdom righteousness is the righteousness that exceeds that of the most religious person, for it is an inward righteousness of a heart where the King reigns. It is not an external observance of rules and regulations, but an expression of the internal reality of a relationship with God through Jesus Christ who is Lord.

FORGIVENESS AND THE KINGDOM
(Luke 15:11–32; Matt. 18:21–35)

Forgiveness was at the heart of Jesus' life and mission.

◈ What words did He utter on the Cross in Luke 23:34?

_____

_____

_____

◈ What do we have through His shed blood? (Eph. 1:7)

_____

_____

◇ Of all the statements in the Lord's Prayer, what subject is amplified at the conclusion of the prayer? What does that tell you of the significance of that subject? (Matt. 6:14, 15)

_____

_____

Jesus used two parables to dramatically demonstrate the forgiving heart of God and to highlight the importance of forgiving others.

1. The Parable of the Lost Son (Luke 15:11–32)

◇ After he came to his senses, what was the attitude of the wayward son? (vv. 18, 19, 21)

_____

_____

◇ How did the father demonstrate his forgiveness and acceptance of his wayward son? (vv. 20, 22–24)

_____

_____

◇ Compare the father's attitude in the parable with the heart of your heavenly Father. What are the similarities? (Luke 15:4–7, 32)

_____

_____

2. The Parable of the Unforgiving Servant (Matt. 18:21–35)

In this passage, we are soberly warned against the human capacity to forget God's gracious gift of forgiveness and allow smallness of soul to breed unforgiveness. Let's first look at Peter's question that caused Jesus to give this parable.

◇ What practical question did Peter ask Jesus? (v. 21)

_____

_____

◇ What was Jesus' answer? (v. 22)

_____

Here, Jesus was emphasizing that forgiveness from the heart does not keep a score of wrongs. Who could keep track of 490 offenses by a brother? True forgiveness is a spirit, not a statistic. Forgiveness "remembers to forget"!

Next, Jesus gives the parable in order to illustrate the blessing of forgiveness and the penalty of unforgiveness. Read the entire parable in Matthew 18:23–35, paying attention to what happened to each servant—the one who had an unpayable debt that was completely out of reach, and the servant who owed only the equivalent of a few months' wages.

◇ How did the master respond to the impassioned plea of his servant who owed a great deal? (v. 27)

_____

◇ The newly-forgiven servant found a fellow-servant who owed him a comparatively small amount of money. What happened? (vv. 28–31)

_____

◇ Since the master was so angry at the first servant's lack of mercy and forgiveness, what did he do to him? (vv. 32–34)

_____

_____

◇ What does verse 35 say about the value of forgiveness in a believer's life?

_____

_____

The master delivered the unforgiving servant to the "torturers" (not simply to prison, but to punishment) until payment was made. This is not legalism or a scare tactic. Rather, it states the seriousness of responsible forgiving and demonstrates how unforgiveness clogs the channel of communication and sanctification between God and His people.

KINGDOM EXTRA

The Greek word for "forgive" in Matthew 18:27, 32 is *aphiemi*. It means to send away, to remit, completely cancel. In reference to the sinner it signifies the remission of punishment, the canceling of sin's penalty or debt. Other places *aphiemi* is used are Matthew 9:2, 5, 6; Romans 4:7; James 5:15; 1 John 1:9.

Another word in the New Testament for forgiveness, *charizomai*, means to do a favor, show kindness unconditionally, give freely, grant forgiveness, forgive freely. The word is from the same root as *charis*, grace. Ephesians 4:32 and Colossians 2:13 use the word *charizomai*.

Heart forgiveness is like God's forgiveness—it is always available when needed. Surely such a spirit of forgiveness must come from the Spirit of God. Unlimited and heartfelt can only come from God Himself—and it has in Christ! And so we are encouraged to treat others as we have been treated. We are to "be kind to one another, tenderhearted, forgiving one another, even as God in Christ forgave you" (Eph. 4:32). Truly, forgiveness starts at the Cross, and forgiveness ends at the Cross.

FAITH ALIVE

◇ What are some things for which God has forgiven you?

◇ Is there someone you need to forgive? If so, go straight to the throne of God in prayer! This does not mean that you excuse or enable bad or hurtful behavior, but it releases you from exacting the penalty. It releases the person to God, and it frees you from harboring resentment or unforgiveness. Having a forgiving heart is essential for your health—spiritually, emotionally, and physically.

◇ Do you have a hard time forgiving? Sometimes the hurts run deep. It's important to stress that forgiveness is a process and may not always be accomplished quickly. After we have forgiven all offenses and hurts we are conscious of, God may reveal a deeper level of pain, as we are emotionally able to handle it, in order to lead us to complete freedom—one step at a time. The point is that we need to: (1) choose to begin the forgiveness process and (2) respond immediately to those new areas of pain that the Lord may surface through time. Then, as we continue to "give it up" to Jesus, its power over our memories will gradually be released until we are no longer tormented by those painful memories of our past experience.

HUMILITY IN THE KINGDOM
(Mark 10:35–45; Luke 22:24–30; John 13:1–17)

"Who is the greatest among us?" On several occasions before Jesus' death, His disciples argued this point. How sad to be caught up in such petty matters as the shadow of the Cross was lengthening over Jesus!

Jesus' response was simple: He came to serve. Greatness is not dominance; it is serving.

Look at Mark 10:35–45 to see how two of Jesus' disciples were jockeying for position. The rest of the disciples were not pleased.

◇ What did James and John want? (v. 37)

_____

◇ Could Jesus answer their request? (vv. 38–40)

_____

◇ How does the world define greatness? (v. 42)

_____

◇ How does Jesus define greatness? (vv. 43, 44)

_____

◇ Why did Jesus come? (v. 45)

_____

Now turn to Luke 22:24–30.

◇ What were the disciples arguing about? (v. 24)

_____

◇ In God's kingdom, who is greater—the younger or the older? The one who governs or the one who submits? The one who sits at the table, or the one who serves? What was Jesus' answer? (vv. 26, 27)

_____

_____

Jesus pointed to Himself as being one among the disciples who served. He then gave them a living example of true greatness as He began to do something unheard of for an honored guest at a meal in that culture—He washed the disciples' feet! Let's read John 13:1–17 and discover what happened, why, and what we are to learn from this fascinating story.

◇ Jesus knew something was going to happen to Him, which made His sacrifice of serving even more poignant. What was about to transpire? (John 13:1–3)

_____

_____

◇ By girding Himself with a servant's towel, Jesus was making the statement that no one should think it beneath his dignity to perform the most menial tasks in serving others. What did He proceed to do? (v. 5)

_____

◇ What happened with Peter, and why did he react like this? (vv. 6–9)

_____

◇ What is the point of the "bathing vs. footwashing" analogy in verses 10 and 11?

_____

◇ What principle was Jesus teaching the disciples? (vv. 14, 15)

_____

◇ Jesus said if you live out the true meaning of greatness through servanthood, you are _____ (v. 17).

"Many who are first will be last, and the last first." With that great statement in Matthew 19:30, Jesus proclaims the message of the kingdom: what counts in God's kingdom is not always appreciated by the world. True greatness of a person doesn't depend upon position, but on willingness to serve. Ability to forgive is far superior to miserliness and meanness of spirit. True righteousness in a person flows from a place of wholeness in right relationship with God.

Not only is Jesus our example, He works His kingdom character in us. Let us not shrink back from being the ones through whom Jesus shines!

FAITH ALIVE

Integrity and rightness of living—the ability to forgive—a heart to serve. Pick one of these areas to focus on this week. Determine to partner with God, asking Him to show you ways you can practically demonstrate growth in one of these areas.

CONFLICT AND VICTORY OF THE KINGDOM

Lesson 8

THE BIG IDEA

Like Alaskan king salmon swimming upstream, we as the King's "fish" (that's our historic symbol) must swim against the tide of the times. Let's move ahead with confidence that the conflict we experience will not deter us from victory in Christ.

JESUS IS VICTOR

When we receive Jesus Christ as Lord and enter God's kingdom, we are transferred from a kingdom of death into a kingdom of life. We now are alive in Christ and destined for a different direction— one directly opposite of "the flow" of this world. (See 1 John 2:15–17.) Jesus Himself faced such an adverse flow and warned His followers that they would face the same opposition—new pressures, tribulation, and persecution. But great reward will come as we experience God's triumph in these things.

As we study the subject of conflict of the kingdom, it is essential to understand that in the coming of Jesus as Messiah, God's kingdom won a decisive victory over the kingdom of darkness. The crushing defeat of death and hell was a massive breaking of sin's power and sin's arch-proponent, Satan. This decisive victory ensures an ultimate victory someday! In the meantime, the intensity of the battle increases. Like a mortally wounded animal, our adversary can be extremely dangerous and tirelessly seeks revenge. Knowing his time is short, he wages intense warfare against God's kingdom and its citizens (Rev. 12:10–12). But we have great assurance that, with Jesus Christ, victory will come.

◈ Read Colossians 1:13, 14. What two opposing things are spoken of here? What is the basis for our position in God's kingdom?

◈ For what reason did the Son of God appear? (1 John 3:8)

◈ When we face conflict, what encouragement does Jesus speak? (1 John 4:4)

◈ What comfort does 1 Corinthians 15:55–57 give?

◈ How do we pray? (Matt. 6:13)

THE AGE-LONG STRUGGLE
(Rev. 12)

Behind the conflict between good and evil in our world is the war between God and Satan in the unseen world. This struggle has been waged since the beginning, even before the serpent in the Garden of Eden contested God's right to rule over His creation. The conflict has continued throughout this age, but with the coming of Jesus Christ, the conflict intensified greatly.

Timeless principles of spiritual warfare are presented in a series of symbolic visions in Revelation 12. These enable us to see the spiritual reality of historical events such as the birth of the Messiah, together with Satan's attempts to destroy Him before He completed His redemptive work, and His exaltation, followed by the resultant persecution of His church. (The symbolism in this chapter is not easy to interpret, but that must not cause us to avoid it. To do so would be to miss the powerful truths it conveys!) We will study Revelation 12 in three sections.

1. Revelation 12:1–6

◈ Who are the two key "players" ("signs") in this conflict? (vv. 1–3)

◈ What did the dragon intend to do to the newborn child? (v. 4)

◇ Why did the dragon intend to do this to the newborn child? (Note how this newborn baby boy is described in v. 5a.)

_____

_____

◇ What happened to the woman's child? (v. 5b)

_____

◇ What happened to the woman? (v. 6)

_____

◇ Look up the following verses about Jesus' life and compare them to the verses you just studied.

A. From the time of His birth when King Herod attempted to kill Him (Matt. 2:13–18),
B. Jesus was in constant danger as even religious leaders attempted to take His life (Mark 3:6).
C. But when it came time for Jesus to die, it was by God's plan and by Jesus' own choice (John 10:18).
D. He died on a cross in Jerusalem as the Lamb of God to take away the sin of the world (John 1:29, 36; 1 Pet. 2:24).
E. Thus, even in death, Satan had no power over Jesus. In fact, the Cross was an unparalleled defeat for Satan and his forces and the Resurrection a decisive blow against the kingdom of darkness as death died and Jesus rose to live forevermore (Col. 2:15; Rev. 1:18).

2. Revelation 12:7–10

◇ Where did war break out, and who were the opponents? (v. 7)

_____

◇ Who won, and what happened to the dragon and his angels? (vv. 8, 9)

_____

_____

◇ As a result of this great "victory," what has now "come"? (v. 10)

_____

Indeed, Satan and his demons have been decisively defeated. The deceiver of "the whole world," the "accuser of our brethren," has been cast down. But heaven's great victory must yet be secured on earth. God's kingdom must yet come on "earth as it is in heaven" (Luke 11:2).

3. Revelation 12:11–17

◈ How did the "brethren" (believers) overcome their "accuser"? (v. 11)

___

◈ What did the devil do when cast to earth? (vv. 12, 13)

___

◈ What happened to the "woman" who gave birth to the male child? (vv. 14–16)

___

◈ What did the frustrated dragon do then? (v. 17)

___

Through the symbolism we see that God won; Satan lost! He lost in his attempt to destroy the male Child, Jesus Christ, the Messiah. Further, he was unable to kill the child's mother (most likely a reference to the true remnant of God's people). Now he attempts to kill the rest of "the woman's offspring" (believers in Jesus Christ). But these are the "overcomers" in verse 11! Look at it, because it's you and me! Again Satan will lose! Throughout the years, there have been many martyrs for the cause of Christ, and there will still be others until He returns; ultimately we all overcome the "dragon" by the blood of the Lamb, and by the word of our testimony.

This is the nature of the age-long conflict between God's kingdom and Satan's kingdom. It is a life-and-death struggle. But in Christ the decisive victory has already been won and the guarantee of ultimate victory secured for God's kingdom and His people. And even though they may suffer and some may even die, the final outcome is certain!

KINGDOM EXTRA

At least three interpretations have been suggested to explain the expulsion of Satan from heaven. We propose they are all true and blend together—like a play with one plot, but three acts or key developments.

The first "casting down" may have occurred before the creation of the heavens and the earth. Isaiah 14:12 speaks of one called "Lucifer, son of the morning," who had "fallen from heaven" and was "cut down to the ground." Ezekiel 28:13–19 describes an "anointed cherub" who was "in Eden, the garden of God" and was "perfect in your ways from the day you were created, till iniquity was found in you." But then due to arrogant pride, this angelic being was "cast ... to the ground." In both passages the descriptions are applied to contemporary wicked rulers apparently through whom Satan himself ruled. Some hold that their "casting down" is a reflection of Satan's own "casting down" before the beginning of creation. As his emissaries their destiny is that of their master.

Second, in Christ's life, death, and Resurrection Satan was "cast down." In Luke 10:18 Jesus told the seventy, upon their return from casting out demons in His name, that He saw "Satan fall like lightning from heaven." Jesus Himself also clearly indicated the reason He cast out demons was because Satan, the "strong man," had been bound (Matt. 12:28, 29).

Third, ultimately Satan, along with the Beast and the False Prophet, is cast into the lake of fire, and their power to deceive is finally and fully destroyed (Rev. 20:10). If these interpretations are correct, the "casting down" of Satan shows his dethroning is that which was, is, and shall be, because God alone is sovereign over all He has made! Further help and insight may be found in such exegetical commentaries as *The Expositor's Greek Testament: the Synoptic Gospels* (Eerdmans, 1979 reprint) and the *New International Greek Testament Commentary on Luke* (Eerdmans, 1978).

SATAN, THE "GOD OF THIS AGE"
(Eph. 2:1–7; 2 Cor. 4:1–6)

Satan's defeat is progressively revealed in the Scriptures and progressively realized during redemptive history. Although decisively defeated and mortally wounded in the Cross and Resurrection of the Messiah, he is the age-long Adversary of God's redemptive purposes until his ultimate destruction in the lake of fire. Until then, Satan continues as the "god of this age." As the ruler of his evil and unrighteous kingdom, he exercises influence globally and within each culture.

◈ In Ephesians 2:1–7, the apostle Paul vividly describes the dramatic contrast between life before and after conversion to Christ. Who did we follow before we were converted to Christ and what was our condition? (vv. 1–3)

_____

_____

◈ What is this contrasted with? (Eph. 2:4–7)

_____

_____

◈ What is Satan's primary strategy as the "god of this age"? (2 Cor. 4:3, 4)

_____

_____

◈ What is the answer to defeating this strategy of Satan? (2 Cor. 4:2, 5, 6)

_____

_____

"In Christ" a person has come under a new Lord. Such a person is liberated from the "god of this age" by the One who alone is the only true King and liberating Lord. His kingdom alone is based on the righteousness of God offered as a free gift to all who humbly repent and truly believe.

JESUS' AUTHORITY OVER SATAN

Scripture declares Jesus' unequivocal victory over Satan and his evil kingdom. Look up each passage and write the truth it states.

Colossians 2:15 _____

_____

Hebrews 2:14, 15 _____

_____

Matthew 4:23, 24 _____

_____

Mark 1:27, 34

_____

Matthew 12:28

_____

It is clear that Jesus could see and operate in the invisible realm. The real battle was not against "flesh and blood" but against spiritual powers (Eph. 6:12). Therefore, the casting out of demons required both the spiritual insight and power that only comes by the Holy Spirit. Such insight and power were evident in the life and ministry of Jesus after the Holy Spirit came upon Him at His baptism in the Jordan (Acts 10:37, 38).

OUR HOPE IN TRIBULATION
(John 16:33; Rev. 12:11)

In Revelation 12, we saw that the kingdom of God has already triumphed over the serpent (vv. 9, 10), yet still, those engaged in conflict in the name of the Lamb suffer hard persecution and are sometimes martyred. How can it be that tribulation coexists in a kingdom where we are also given God's joy, peace, and Holy Spirit empowered authority?

We know that Jesus was opposed and rejected, yet triumphed at the Cross. Like He was, we will be hated and persecuted (John 15:18–20). Jesus said, "In the world you will have tribulation; but be of good cheer, I have overcome the world" (John 16:33). Let's check out the Word Wealth meaning for "tribulation."

Tribulation, _thlipsis_ (John 16:33). Pressure, oppression, stress, anguish, tribulation, adversity, affliction, crushing, squashing, squeezing, distress. Imagine placing your hand on a stack of loose items and manually compressing them. That is _thlipsis_, putting a lot of pressure on that which is free and unfettered. _Thlipsis_ is like spiritual bench-pressing. The word is used of crushing grapes or olives in a press.

◈ A key word in our definition is "press." When grapes are pressed, are they totally destroyed? Look up 2 Corinthians 4:8, 9 before answering.

_____

❖ What will happen to those who "desire to live godly in Christ Jesus"? (2 Tim. 3:12)

_____

_____

❖ Knowing what to expect better prepares people to face the future with faith. To be forewarned is to be forearmed! How does 1 Thessalonians 3:3, 4 demonstrate this principle?

_____

_____

Conflict and the kingdom of God are integrally related. Light has come into darkness, and the darkness seeks to quench it. Life has come into the realm of death, and death seeks to conquer it. However, in the Son of God was life, and the life was "the light of men. And the light shines in the darkness and the darkness did not comprehend [overcome] it" (John 1:4, 5). Instead, the Light is overcoming the darkness, for the Life has conquered death. "For as in Adam all die, even so in Christ all shall be made alive . . . for He must reign till He has put all enemies under His feet" (1 Cor. 15:22, 25).

❖ What is the last enemy to be destroyed? (1 Cor. 15:26)

_____

❖ What comes after tribulation? (John 16:33)

_____

❖ Look again at Revelation 12:11. How is Satan overcome?

_____

_____

FAITH ALIVE

❖ The presence of the King and the power of His kingdom in our lives make us neither invulnerable nor immune to life's struggles. But they do bring the promise of victory! How can we find balance in our faith, pressing into victory in the face of conflict? Use some of the verses we studied in this lesson to help you form your answer.

_____

_____

_____

_____

_____

_____

_____

◇ Declare your abiding faith in the accomplished work of the Cross. Participate in Jesus' ultimate victory, overcoming Satan by the power of the Cross and the steadfastness of your confession of faith in Christ's triumph!

_____

_____

_____

_____

_____

_____

INTRODUCTION: THE KINGDOM: PAST, PRESENT AND FUTURE
Part Two

With these words, "The kingdom of God is at hand," Jesus Christ ushered in a new era of God's kingdom rule. He brought the reality of the kingdom to our hearts, and we have been impacted by it. Through Him, we have obtained citizenship in His heavenly kingdom, a rich heritage, and the sure promise of a bright and wonderful future!

There is so much to see in the kingdom of God! In this section we will look at the full-orbed spectrum of the kingdom as it relates to our history as a human race, our spiritual heritage, and prophetic revelation in God's Word. This will involve indepth study that covers a broad historical time period. Much of this will be from the Old Testament.

Why is it important to study the past and the future of the kingdom in relationship to the present?

1. If we can understand the Fall of man and his continuing failure, then we will see how badly we *need* God's kingdom rule and that human effort *cannot produce* it!

2. The fact that prophets *foretold* the kingdom confirms its reality, because what they said happened—and *will* happen.

3. We can learn much from the Jewish *expectation* of the coming Messiah and from God's *dealings* with the Jews.

4. To be able to perceive the coming kingdom through prophetic insight gives us <u>hope</u> in our current circumstances to <u>anticipate</u> the kingdom's full consummation.

Let's gird up our minds and move into strong truth, presenting and balancing the vital truth of the kingdom of God. We will start in Genesis.

THE KINGDOM IN GENESIS
Lesson 9

THE BIG IDEA

Kingdom rule—kingdom lost—kingdom hope! This summarizes what happened in the kingdom in the beginning. As you trace the kingdom's history through Genesis, you will discover foundational truth that has great impact upon your faith—today!

GOD'S SOVEREIGNTY, MAN'S RESPONSIBILITY
(Gen. 1; 2)

The beginning point in studying the theme of the kingdom of God is in the Bible's opening verse. Here, we are introduced to the sovereignty of God, Creator of the heavens and the earth.

Write out Genesis 1:1.

_____

_____

_____

_____

There are two accounts of creation in the Bible, which when studied together complement one another and fill out our understanding (Gen. 1:1—2:3; 2:4–25). We will take a look at both of them.

1. Genesis 1:1—2:3

◇ Write down what happens each time God speaks. As you do this, you will see that the focus is on God's sovereign, creative power and the authority of His Word.

1:3 _____

_____

1:6 _____

_____

1:9

_____

1:10

_____

1:14

_____

1:20

_____

1:24

_____

1:26

_____

Note God's majestic might, His unique power, His creative wisdom—all come thundering through. There is none who even comes close to His awesome greatness. God alone is Creator. He alone is the Source of all that exists. He alone sustains that which He has made. Therefore, every created thing owes its existence to Him.

◇ What does God think about what He created? What does that tell us about what kind of God He is? (Gen. 1:31)

_____

_____

2. Genesis 2:4–25

This second account of creation expands the story of the creation of humankind, the last and highest creation of God. The account begins where the first account left off—with man's creation in his Maker's own image.

◇ What does God do in each of these verses?

2:7

_____

2:8

_____

◊ Re-read Genesis 1:26, 27. How is the image/likeness of God described in these verses?

The creation account clearly indicates that God is the Creator of all. As the Source of all life, it is evident He alone is sovereign, "in charge." His benevolent intent in creating things "good" reveals His holy nature, and thus His moral right to be creation's King. All kingdom power and authority flow from Him.

The Sovereign Lord of the universe makes a choice to delegate to man "dominion . . . on the earth." Man's power and authority for exercising this rule originate in God's intent to make man in His own "image" and "likeness" (Gen. 1:26–28). Let's study what is meant by "dominion." List the human duties of delegated dominion in the following verses.

Genesis 1:28

Genesis 2:15

Genesis 2:19, 20

Did God give man any other responsibility? (Gen. 2:16, 17)

God said "Let Us make man in Our image, according to Our likeness." He created man to be His "kingdom agent," to rule and subdue the rest of creation. This includes the aggressive satanic forces, which will infringe upon it.

MAN'S PROBATION AND PRESUMPTION
(Gen. 3:1–11)

Up to this point, we have seen that man's unique made-in-the-image-of-God nature gave him the "right" or the authority to rule over creation (Gen. 1:26–28). He was to "tend and keep" God's garden, the Garden of Eden (Gen. 2:15). He was allowed to eat freely of every tree of the garden, including the Tree of Life. But of the fruit of one tree, man was not to eat.

⟡ Why do you think God made one tree "off limits"? (Gen. 2:16, 17)

⟡ What do you think is represented by "the tree of the knowledge of good and evil"? (Gen. 2:9)

⟡ What was God prohibiting from man? (Gen. 3:6, 22.)

⟡ If people were not to know "good and evil" by firsthand experience, then how were they to know it? Why?

As God's responsible agent to tend, care, and rule over creation, man was put on "probation" by his Creator and Master, but he blew it! Just one prohibition, and Adam and Eve could not pass the test of obedience. Rather than focusing on all they could enjoy, they were tempted by the Serpent to focus on the one thing that was forbidden. Using doubt and deception, the Tempter asked, "Has God indeed said?" and claimed, "You will not surely die" (Gen. 3:1, 4). Thus, the man and woman succumbed to the Serpent's cunning strategy and ate the "forbidden fruit." The underlying issue was trust. Would they believe and trust God and His word, or would they believe and trust the Tempter's word? Tragically, they chose the latter. They sinned, disobeying God's command and violating His trust in them as His ruling agents over creation.

IMPACT OF SIN
(Gen. 3:7–24)

The result of humankind's unbelief and disobedience was devastating!

1. Innocence was *lost*. Nakedness became an embarrassment (Gen. 2:25; 3:7).

2. Their relationship with their Creator became characterized by *guilt* rather than joy, and so they attempted to *hide* from Him (Gen. 3:8).

3. When God called to Adam and asked, "Where are you?" the response was one of *fear* (Gen. 3:9, 10).

4. Such fear resulted in defensive *rationalizations* for their disobedience when asked what they had done (Gen. 3:11–13).

Take a moment and look at Adam and Eve's rationalizations. What does each rationalization wrongfully imply about God?

◈ The man's answer (Gen. 3:12)

_____

_____

◈ The woman's answer (Gen. 3:13)

_____

_____

God's answer was to spell out "the wages of [their] sin" (Rom. 6:23). Look at the judgments that were pronounced on the Tempter, the woman, and the man in Genesis 3:14–19.

◈ What was the judgment upon the Serpent? (vv. 14, 15)

_____

_____

◈ What was the judgment upon the woman? (v. 16)

_____

_____

◈ What was the judgment upon the man? (vv. 17–19)

_____

_____

Notice that although only the Serpent is directly "cursed," that which was originally intended as blessings for the woman and man now become burdens. In a sense, they become a "curse." Greatly increased sorrow and pain will now characterize childbearing, and the husband will rule over the wife. Because the ground is "cursed" with thorns and thistles, man's working of the soil now becomes characterized by sweat and toil until the day he dies. The most dramatic "wage" for their sin was to be driven out of the Garden of Eden (Gen. 3:22–24).

Was God right? Did Adam and Eve "die" the day they ate of the forbidden fruit? List the immediate, eventual, and ultimate effects of "the Fall" as recorded in Genesis 3.

immediate effects (vv. 7–13)

eventual effects (vv. 14–20)

ultimate effects (vv. 21–24)

Thus, through disobedience to the terms of his rule, man falls, experiencing the loss of his dominion (Gen. 3:22, 23). Everything of his delegated realm (earth) comes under a curse as his relationship with God, the fountainhead of his power to rule, is severed (vv. 17, 18). Thus man loses the "life" power essential to ruling in God's kingdom (vv. 19, 22).

Beyond the tragedy of man's loss, two other sobering facts unfold. First, through his disobedience to God and submission to the Serpent's suggestions, man's rule has been forfeited to the Serpent. Revelation 12:9 verifies that the spirit employing the snake's form was Satan himself. The domain originally delegated to man now falls to Satan, who becomes administrator of this now-cursed realm. The Serpent's "seed" and "head" indicate a continual line (seed) of evil offspring extending Satan's rule (head) (Gen. 3:15). However, a second fact offers hope. Amid the tragedy of this sequence of events, God begins to move redemptively, and a plan for recovering man's lost estate is promised (3:15) and set in motion with the first sacrifice (3:21).

THE "FALLOUT" OF THE FALL
(Gen. 4—11)

Sadly, the deadly impact of sin's failure continued in Adam and Eve's descendents.

◇ What happened to Adam and Eve's son, Abel? (Gen. 4:8)

◇ To underscore that the "wages of sin are death" (Rom. 6:23), what happened to Adam? (Gen. 5:5)

◇ What tragic thing was said of each of Adam's descendents throughout the fifth chapter of Genesis?

◇ By the time of Noah, the wickedness of humankind was great. What did the Lord say about making man? (Gen. 6:6)

◇ Through what event did God visit judgment on humankind? (Gen. 6:17; 7:17–24)

◇ Noah's family and the animals they brought with them survived the Flood through God's provision of the ark. But Noah's descendents reverted to pagan ways. What did they try to do that revealed their pride and quest for self-rule? (Gen. 11:4)

GOD'S MERCY
(Gen. 3:15, 21–24; 8:21, 22)

Up to this point the picture is very dark. But in the midst of judgment is mercy! God's justice is only understood in the context of His love. He is a compassionate Creator. He is merciful in His might. His rules are only understood in light of His relationships, for He is a Creator who deeply desires fellowship with His creation made in His image. It was God who sought out the man and woman when they sinned (Gen. 3:8, 9). See if you can discover the "light in the midst of the darkness."

◇ Out of His *unending love*, what did God promise in Genesis 3:15?

◇ Out of His *undeserved mercy*, what did God provide for Adam and Eve in Genesis 3:21?

◈ Out of His *amazing kindness*, why did God drive Adam and Eve from the Garden? (Gen. 3:22–24)

___

◈ Out of His *great compassion*, what did God promise after He spared Noah and his family in Genesis 8:21, 22?

___

Sin is not the end. It is but the beginning of God's rescue plan of redemption and restoration!

GOD'S COVENANT TO ABRAHAM
(Gen. 17:1–13)

We now come to a major turning point in God's redemptive work for human salvation and restoration. Although God's mercy is evident in the earliest chapters of Genesis, it is not until we come to Abram (later Abraham) that we see clearly God's redemptive choice of a man through whom He will bless and rescue humankind from their unbelief, disobedience, and rebellion against their Creator (Gen. 12).

◈ Turn to Genesis 12:1–3. What did God tell Abram to do? (v. 1)

___

◈ List the blessings God promised Abram if he were obedient. (12:2, 3)

___

◈ Were such blessings to be restricted only to Abram and his descendants? Who else would receive blessing? (12:3)

___

◈ But there is more! To and through whom else were such multiple and widespread blessings directly promised? (Gen. 26:1–5; 28:10–14)

___

The God of Abraham, Isaac, and Jacob is the God who desires to bless all the families of the earth with far more than material blessings. He desires to bless them with Himself. This He expresses in the form of His everlasting covenant beginning in Genesis 17.

◈ What does God promise to establish for Abraham and his descendants? (17:7)

The word "covenant" has significant meaning. Let's take a look.

WORD WEALTH

Covenant, *berit* (Gen. 17:7). A covenant, compact, pledge, treaty, agreement. This is one of the most theologically important words in the Bible, appearing more than 250 times in the Old Testament. A *berit* may be made between individuals, between a king and his people, or by God with His people. Here God's irrevocable pledge is that He will be God to Abraham and his descendants forever. The greatest provision of the Abrahamic covenant, this is the foundation stone of Israel's eternal relationship to God, a truth affirmed by David (2 Sam. 7:24), by the Lord Himself (Jer. 33:24–26), and by Paul (Rom. 9:4; 11:2, 29). All other Bible promises are based on this one.

◈ What is a covenant?

◈ According to this Word Wealth, what is unique about the covenant God made with Abraham in Genesis 17:7?

◈ What are the terms of God's covenant with Abraham? (Gen. 17:1–13)

◇ God's covenant includes an amazing promise. This is clearly seen in God's reason for delivering Abraham's descendants, the nation of Israel, out of bondage in Egypt. Look at Exodus 29:45, 46. What does God promise?

_____

_____

◇ The fullness of the blessing God made to Abraham is that which shall ultimately characterize God's kingdom. This is powerfully described in Revelation 21 and 22. What does Revelation 21:3 say?

_____

_____

God intends through Abraham and his offspring to restore that which was lost in the Fall. He promised to Abraham and his descendants:

Headship—"I will be God to you"
Relationship—"You will be My people"
Fellowship—"I will dwell among you"

Abraham believed in the Lord, and "it was accounted to him for righteousness" (Rom. 4:22; see Gen. 15:6). Abraham thus becomes the prototype of all who experience God's processes of seeking to reinstate man through redemption, first and foremost, in his relationship to God by faith, without works (Rom. 4:1–25). We do not know why God chose Abraham, who formerly was from a pagan, idol-worshiping society, but we know that through Abraham, God displayed His grace and love.

OUR LESSON FROM GENESIS

The "kingdom" concept of God's delegating His rule on earth to be administered through those who walk with Him is birthed at creation. Although damaged at man's Fall, it is progressively being reinstated as a redemptive goal and is demonstrated in those who accept His covenant. For it is through Jesus Christ, "the Son of David, the Son of Abraham" (Matt. 1:1), that God's kingdom will come.

◈ How does "kingdom rule—kingdom lost—kingdom hope" describe what you just studied? (Before answering, it might be helpful for you to turn to the summary of this lesson, "Old Testament Background of the Kingdom," found in Appendix A, #1–6.)

_____

_____

_____

FAITH ALIVE

◈ What have you learned about the Fall and its aftermath that relates to your relationship to Christ?

_____

_____

◈ What hope does the covenant given to Abraham give you today?

_____

_____

KINGDOM HERITAGE
Lesson 10

THE BIG IDEA

God's redemptive love. The thread of this theme winds its way through the priests, kings, and prophets of the Old Testament, adding depth to our understanding of the kingdom. Allow the substance and fabric of your life to be strengthened as you discover the wisdom of God's unfolding plan through His people in spite of their failures.

KINGDOM OF PRIESTS
(Ex. 19:3–6)

"You shall be to Me a kingdom of priests and a holy nation" (Ex. 19:6). With these words, the Lord God indicates His objective for His delivered people.

Let's start by looking at the ones who performed priestly duties, the Levites. They were called to be the priests and assistants to the priests in the worship by the nation of Israel. As God's "intermediaries" for His people, their priestly ministry was carried out on behalf of the other twelve tribes of Israel.

Scripture tells us that when the Levites stood up for the Lord and were obedient to Him, Moses declared to them, "Consecrate yourselves today to the LORD, that He may bestow on you a blessing this day" (Ex. 32:29). Subsequently, the Levites became known as the "priestly tribe" (Josh. 18:7). What were the functions of the priests according to these passages?

Exodus 29:42–46
_____

_____

Exodus 30:7–10
_____

_____

_____

This Word Wealth will help to enrich your understanding of the function and place of the priest.

WORD WEALTH

Priest, *kohen* (Lev. 5:6). A priest; especially a chief priest; a minister, a personal attendant, an officer; specifically the high priest descended from Aaron. The *kohen* was the Lord's "personal attendant," one whose entire life revolved around Yahweh's service, both through ministering in the tabernacle (or temple in later times) and in carrying the burden of the people of Israel (Ex. 28:29). A *kohen* ministers to the Lord as priest (Ex. 28:1). Notice the six appearances of the words "minister," "serve," or "service" in the references to the high priest in Hebrews 8:1—9:10. To this day the Jewish surname "Cohen" identifies a family descended from Aaron the high priest.

◇ What was to be the priest's entire focus?

_____

_____

Now turn to Exodus 19:3–6. This is the first time the words *kingdom* and *priests* are tied together in the Old Testament.

◇ Write out the first sentence of verse 6. Who is to become this "kingdom of priests"?

_____

_____

Why a "nation of priests" when they had a "tribe of priests"? Could it be that what the tribe of Levi did for the nation of Israel, the entire nation of Israel was to do for the nations? What do these passages say about Israel's relationship to the nations?

2 Chronicles 6:32, 33
_____

_____

Isaiah 2:2, 3
_____

_____

Isaiah 49:6
_____

_____

Look at another phrase in Exodus 19:6. In addition to being a kingdom of priests, they were to be a *holy* nation. If they were to represent the God of Israel before the nations, they must be distinct and different from those nations. They were to be holy, like their God. Their worship was to be pure. Idolatry must never characterize this "holy nation." The people are different because the true and living God is the focus of their lives.

◇ What were the *conditions* and *blessings* for being a holy nation and kingdom of priests? (Ex. 19:5)

_____

_____

Above all else God desired Israel's worship, for it was out of the witness of their worship that surrounding nations would come to know the only true and living God, the "Holy One of Israel." It is God's intention that as His people learn to worship as a nation of priests, they will discover His foundational means for their possessing their future victories as ones whose domain, or "kingdom," He has promised.

◇ It is exciting to realize that in the New Testament we are called a "chosen generation, a royal priesthood, a holy nation." What are we to proclaim? (1 Pet. 2:9)

_____

FAITH ALIVE

What are the implications of your being called "a royal priesthood"? What does that tell you about the importance of worship in your life?

OLD TESTAMENT BACKGROUND OF THE KINGDOM

In order to understand the *value* of the kingdom, one needs to understand the *climate* into which Jesus proclaimed the kingdom. This requires extensive historical study of the Old Testament events that provided the backdrop and context of the message of the kingdom. The purpose of the rest of this chapter will be to highlight historical events that demonstrate the Jews' desperate need of a messiah to bring the kingdom. These will be presented in a "summary-type" format (more reading, less questions to answer). As you read, sit back and absorb the general flow of events.

1. *The people reject God's rule and favor human rule* (1 Sam. 8—10; 2 Sam. 7:1-17).

God Himself was to be Israel's King. But Israel proved to be disloyal, a wayward nation to their King. Often they served other "gods" who were not gods at all (Deut. 7:16). Eventually God's intended theocracy (God-ruled) became a monarchy (man-ruled) when God's people demanded a king to judge them like all the other nations (1 Sam. 8:5).

With strong warnings, God consented to the people's demands and gave them King Saul through whom God would rule His people (1 Sam. 8:9-22; 10:17-25). But Saul did not carry out God's commands. Saul, who had begun so humbly, disqualified himself as king. So God removed His anointing to rule from Saul and chose and anointed as king a shepherd boy, David, "a man after His own heart" (1 Sam.13:14; 1 Sam. 16:1-13). Through King David and his descendants, God said He would establish a lasting kingdom (2 Sam. 7:16).

2. *The kingdom splits* (1 Kin. 11:1—12:20).

Unfortunately, David's son Solomon had married women from the surrounding nations to secure his kingdom. These wives turned his heart away from the true, living God to false gods (1 Kin. 11:1-4). The people became increasingly immersed in gross sin and idolatry. As a result, God said that the kingdom would be torn away from Solomon (1 Kin. 11:9-13). When this happened, ten tribes defected to the north (Israel), leaving only one tribe (Judah) in the south.

The long, sad tale of these two kingdoms was largely one of persistent and pervasive idolatry. Of the nineteen kings in the northern kingdom of Israel, not one was considered a good king. Meanwhile in Judah, only eight of twenty were identified as good kings. (1 Kin. 12:1—22:53; 2 Kin.; 2 Chr. 10:1—36:16).

3. *The kingdoms are taken captive* (2 Kin. 17:6-41; 25:1-21).

The thread of human failure continued throughout the history of God's people. Instead of their worship and service being a light to the nations and a witness to the true and living God, they were polluted and their witness deceptive. Rather than converting these nations to the one and true living God, God's people themselves were converted to the worship of other gods.

In time, God used pagan nations as instruments of His righteous judgment. In 722 B.C., the Assyrians defeated, deported, and dispersed the northern tribes of Israel (2 Kin. 17:6–41). The purpose of this tactic by the enemy was to completely destroy Israel's identity as a nation.

For a season, God spared Judah the same fate as Israel's in response to King Hezekiah's humility and prayer. (This story is told in Is. 36 and 37; 2 Kin. 18:17—19:37; 2 Chr. 32:1–23.) But Judah's judgement was only delayed. Increasing idolatry brought about her eventual judgement through defeat by the Babylonians in 586 B.C. (2 Kin. 25:1–21). The Babylonians defeated and deported Judah, but they did not disperse the people like the Assyrians had the northern tribes. Thus, the Lord preserved a remnant of His people through whom His saving purpose could continue. The apostle Paul states that had not God preserved a remnant of the physical Israel, the entire apostate nation would have been wiped out (Rom. 9:27).

KINGDOM EXTRA

We see within the Old Testament a growing transformation of the hope of the coming kingdom of God. The prophet Daniel lived during the time of the Babylonian captivity. Through visions of human kingdoms replaced by God's eternal kingdom, he presented an alternative to the popular hope of a human deliverer after the line of David (Dan. 2, 7). This divine kingdom is brought by "One like the Son of Man" who comes from heaven (Dan. 7:13, 14). Such visions were the seed for the apocalyptic hope of God's inbreaking into human history from above. Helpful insights into this significant transformation can be found in George E. Ladd's *A New Testament Theology*, pages 68–69 (Eerdmans, 1974). Also, more information on Daniel's visions is given in chapter 12 of this study guide.

4. *A remnant is restored* (Ezra, Nehemiah).

Three prophets had anticipated Judah's deliverance from captivity in Babylon—Isaiah (Is. 45:1–13), Jeremiah (Jer. 25:12; 29:10–14), and Daniel (Dan. 9:1–19).

The promise of Judah's deliverance was fulfilled when Zerubbabel led 50,000 exiles to Jerusalem to rebuild the temple (Ezra 1—2). Proper worship of the God of Israel was reinstituted (Ezra 3:1—6:22).

Ezra led another group of exiles to Jerusalem (Ezra 7:1—8:36). Purified from their idolatrous ways, the exiles conscientiously sought to please the Lord. Led by Ezra and later by Nehemiah, the people took on numerous reforms (Ezra 9:1—10:44; Neh. 5:1-12; 13:1-31).

5. *The coming day of the Lord* (Mal. 3; 4).

Even though the people tried to make some reforms and follow the Law, it wasn't enough; their attempts did not bring God's presence or justice. The people needed more! They needed the Deliverer Himself promised to the prophets. Then, God spoke through the prophet Malachi. God told the people that He would send His messenger to prepare the way for God's coming. This "forerunner" of Christ has been linked to John the Baptist. God also told them that a second Messenger would come, "the Messenger of the covenant" (3:1). With this final chapter in the Old Testament, the people began to anticipate the coming "day of the Lord" (Mal. 4:1-6).

6. *God is silent for four hundred years* (Amos 8:11, 12).

Malachi gave the last prophetic word from God around 430 B.C. Thus begins what is known as the "four hundred silent years." From the time of Malachi to John the Baptist there was no living word from the Lord to His people. Prophetic inspiration ceased. The God of Israel was silent. This period of silence had been prophesied years before by the prophet Amos. As he had predicted, there was a "famine . . . of hearing the words of the LORD" (Amos 8:11, 12).

7. *The Jews interpret God's silence by developing ideas that would shape their view of God's coming kingdom.*

In an attempt to meet this desperate desire to hear a word from God, so-called "apocalyptic writers" (from the Greek *apocalypsis*, meaning "revelation") offered their interpretation of God's silence. Their words were supposedly based on "revelations" that explained why evil seemed to triumph and how God's kingdom would intervene shortly to vindicate the righteous. Yes, God might no longer directly be speaking and actively working in history, said the apocalyptists, but that would all change in the near future. They claimed God's righteous kingdom would come from above and put an end to all evil earthly kingdoms. The wicked nations would be judged and God's righteous nation rewarded.

The prophetic hope of the Old Testament was slowly transformed from one of largely historical and earthly dimensions to one of primarily apocalyptic and heavenly dimensions. The increasing evil of the intertestamental period seemed to rule out the establishment of God's kingdom through merely an historical and earthly king. Only the divine intervention of God Himself from above could bring His kingdom to earth. Only the coming of God's own righteous kingdom could put an end to evil human kingdoms.

God's chosen people considered themselves righteous, for they were now keeping the Law of Moses. Since only the Jews in Israel were close enough to travel to the temple in Jerusalem for worship, the study of the Law became the major focus in the synagogues dispersed throughout the Mediterranean world. In fact, in order to make sure no transgression of God's law occurred, Jewish religious leaders built "a fence around the Law." Oral laws interpreted how to properly keep the written laws found in the books of Moses. And it was the Pharisees who were the most conscientious in attempting to keep all the laws, both written and oral. The result of such a growing emphasis on the Law among the Jews was a *stifling legalism that made keeping the Law, rather than God's gracious covenant, the basis of relationship with God.* Keeping "the rules" became more important than loving God and people.

READY TO RECEIVE

History shows us that humankind had failed to follow God. The word of the Lord that proclaimed "You shall be to Me a kingdom of priests and a holy nation" (Ex. 19:6) was not happening in His people's experience. The word of the Lord was scarce. People wondered, "Where is the God of justice?" Such conditions made the people ready to receive the kingdom's message of repentance from John the Baptist, and from the Lord Himself.

◈ In this lesson there has been much information for you to process! Re-read each of the seven overview statements. (Also, you may wish to turn to a summary of this lesson, "Old Testament Background of the Kingdom," found in Appendix A, #7–12.)

◈ Choose one of the historical periods to study more in depth.

1. Look up some or all of the Scriptures given.

_____

_____

_____

2. Try to put yourself into the mindset of that historical period.

_____

_____

3. Ask yourself what happened during this time that con-
tributed to the great need of the people to receive their messiah.

_____

_____

4. Then write a brief summary of your own about what happened to the Jewish people in that historical period.

_____

_____

_____

FAITH ALIVE

Can you see how the minds of the Jewish people were shaped
into expecting deliverance through a human kingdom? What les-
sons from this chapter can you bring to your life during the times
you are experiencing dry seasons of your own? What is your hope?

THE KINGDOM—NOW/NOT YET

Lesson 11

THE BIG IDEA

How can the kingdom be here ("The kingdom of God is at hand")—yet be promised for the future? In this lesson you will unravel this seeming enigma!

THE END OF AN ERA

Things looked pretty bleak. God's people had been plundered by the superpowers of the day. In addition, it had been a long time since God last spoke. People were asking God, "Why do You wait to deliver us?" Then after four hundred silent years, the "famine" of not hearing the word of the Lord was broken. It happened through a most unusual man—John the Baptist.

◇ What was John's message? (Matt. 3:2)

_____

◇ Who did John say he was? (Compare Matt. 3:3 with Is. 40:3 to answer this question.)

_____

◇ What did John do? (Matt. 3:5, 6)

_____

A hinge point in history occurred with John the Baptist. An era of divine silence and inactivity ended. God was speaking and acting! To appreciate the true significance of this amazing man, look at what Jesus Himself said about John the Baptist.

◇ How did Jesus describe John? (Matt. 11:7–10)

_____

_____

◇ What did God's messenger do? (Matt. 11:10; see also Mal. 3:1)

_____

_____

◇ What did Jesus say ended with John? (Matt. 11:13)

_____

◇ Who did Jesus say John really was? (Matt. 11:14; 17:10–13; see also Mal. 4:5, 6)

_____

_____

If John the Baptist is indeed the Elijah who is to come, then the "day of the Lord" must be near (Mal. 4:5, 6). And if this is so, then proper preparation for this great "day" was essential.

◇ What did John say was required of all who would "prepare the way of the Lord"? (Luke 3:3)

_____

◇ Write what would be the result of honest repentance:

1. for the Jewish people (Luke 3:7–11)

_____

_____

2. for tax collectors (Luke 3:12, 13)

_____

_____

3. for soldiers (Luke 3:14)

_____

_____

4. for families (Luke 1:17)

_____

_____

John was saying that a profound rearrangement of priorities was required. Right relationships and caring about people must take precedence over one's own interests. This was the kind of "fruit" of repentance that prepared the way for God to act.

The long, drought finally ended! No longer did God's people have to endure the guesses of the apocalyptists. God Himself was again speaking. His kingdom was near because the King was here in fulfillment of Old Testament Scriptures. The sad fact is that most of the Jews missed the kingdom because their anticipation was of a king who would set up a physical kingdom right then. What many people fail to see is that the kingdom is two-edged and relates to two frames of time. We experience it now, yet anticipate its full consummation.

THE PRESENT AND FUTURE KINGDOM

An important key in understanding Jesus' view of the kingdom is to understand His view of redemptive history. Jesus understood there were two ages: this present age and the age to come (Matt. 12:32; Luke 18:29, 30; John 12:25). But Jesus had a view of the kingdom that seemed to integrate both the prophetic view and the apocalyptic view found in the Old Testament in such passages as Isaiah 9:6, 7 and Daniel 7:13, 14. The kingdom of God would involve both earthly and heavenly dimensions. As a result, Jesus seemed to indicate the kingdom was both here and not here. It was both present and yet promised. Take a look at each of these passages and write down that which is both available now and yet is still in the future, noting especially the contrast between the present and future tenses of the verbs:

COMPARE	PRESENT (NOW)	FUTURE (NOT YET)
Matthew 8:11 and 21:31, 32		
Matthew 5:6, 10 and 7:21		

COMPARE	PRESENT (NOW)	FUTURE (NOT YET)
Matthew 5:19, 20 and 6:33		
Luke 19:9 and Matthew 10:22		
John 5:25 and 5:28, 29		
John 3:14–16 and Luke 5:29, 30		

Jesus taught that the kingdom and its blessings are available now, and yet they are promised in the future. Thus, a "now, not yet" tension seems to exist about the kingdom. The kingdom is today, yet it is also tomorrow. The kingdom is present, yet promised. Fulfillment of the Old Testament hope without apocalyptic consummation seems to be Jesus' view of redemptive history. It represents a radical modification of the views of His "contemporaries."

KINGDOM EXTRA

Jesus taught that the future righteous age of God's rule has come into this age in an unexpected manner. The kingdom of God is now, yet it is future. Such a perspective is called "eschatological dualism." The future eschatological age (Greek, *eschaton*, "last things") has invaded this present age, making available the blessings of the future age now—at least in part. Thus an "overlap of the ages" has occurred. Two ages are occurring simultaneously. And this has happened because something significant has taken place. The King has come! Thus, the kingdom has come.

The discussion about the kingdom of God as present or future, earthly or heavenly, political or spiritual, ideal or real, now or not yet, continues. Literature on the subject abounds. Several books focus the issues in a most helpful manner. For further study several books are recommended. These are considered to be "classics" on the subject: John Bright, *The Kingdom of God* (Abingdon Press, 1953); E. Stanley Jones, *The Unshakable Kingdom and the Unchangeable Person* (Abingdon Press, 1972); George E. Ladd, *The Gospel of the Kingdom* (Eerdmans, 1959).

THE TIME IS FULFILLED
(Mark 1:15)

Jesus said, "The *time* is fulfilled, and the kingdom of God is at hand. Repent and believe in the gospel" (Mark 1:15). He is saying that the kingdom is accessible (at hand), and the time is now—present-tense now (the "*kairos*" time is fulfilled). Let's look at the Greek translation for "time" as Jesus used it here.

WORD WEALTH

Time, *kairos* (Col. 4:5). Opportune time, set time, appointed time, due time, definitive time, seasonable time, proper time for action. *Kairos* describes kind, or quality, of time, whereas *chronos* denotes extent, or quantity of time.

Clearly, the note of fulfillment is evident in Jesus' proclamation. The word He used, *kairos*, points toward a set season and calls for a proper response, because the time of fulfillment ("filling full") has arrived. The kingdom of God has drawn near. Jesus was the One whose coming occasioned this time of "fulfillment" because He was the One who brought the kingdom as the messianic king of David's line. Thus the coming of the Messiah, Jesus Christ, brought a special "*kairos* moment" which demanded an appropriate response.

◇ By using *kairos*, Jesus is saying now is the proper time for action. What action is called for in Mark 1:15? What is to be our response?

_____

_____

SPIRIT-FILLED LIFE® STUDY GUIDE

LIVING AND ANTICIPATING THE KINGDOM
(Luke 17:20–30)

"The kingdom of God is at hand" declared Jesus. But how <u>near</u> is "at hand"? Jesus taught that the kingdom had come in fulfillment of the Old Testament hope, but without full consummation, which was yet future. Although God's salvation through His anointed Messiah was one act—His act—it would be played out in two scenes upon the stage of human history. And so the Messiah came the first time almost incognito as a suffering Servant in anticipation of His Second Coming in triumphant glory as "King of kings and Lord of lords." The Lion of the tribe of Judah came first as the Lamb of God to take away the sin of the world. Thus, "at hand" really consisted of *two* hands. God's kingdom would "come near" at two moments in history.

◈ Let's take a close look at Luke 17:20–30 to study these two moments. When asked by the Pharisees "when the kingdom of God would come," how did Jesus answer? (Luke 17:20, 21)

_____

_____

_____

What does this mean? The nature of the kingdom is such that it can sneak up on you. It does not come "with observation." In fact, it is "within" or "in the midst of" you. Whether the meaning of the word is "in you" or "among you," the point is clear. God's kingdom is not an outward, visible, observable kingdom as had been anticipated by the Jews. Thus, it could be "at hand" or "near" and be missed.

Jesus then explained to His disciples about another future coming of the kingdom "when the Son of Man is revealed" (Luke 17:30). "But first He must suffer many things and be rejected by this generation" (v. 25). Then there would come a "day" of the Son of Man that would be as observable as the Flood in Noah's day and the destruction of Sodom and Gomorrah in Lot's day. And although false prophets would lead some people astray, apparently for the watchful and discerning person there would be "signs" that would enable them to prepare properly for this "[day] of the Son of Man" (vv. 23, 24).

◈ Look at Luke 17:26–30 and list the common characteristics of their days with the day when the Son of Man is revealed.

1. "As it was in the days of Noah"

_____

_____

_____

2. "As it was also in the days of Lot"

_____

_____

_____

What seems to be the focus of the things described by Jesus? Is it on the dramatic increase of wickedness or the undramatic continuation of normal life-activities? If it is the latter, which it probably is, then the Second Coming of the Messiah could sneak up on people as did the Flood and Sodom's destruction. How can such observable and dramatic events catch people off guard? It is because they missed "hearing the voice of God" calling them to prepare before these great events occurred. It is because they missed "first comings" that they were unprepared for the "Second Coming." The Scripture is clear: God "does nothing, unless He reveals His secret to His servants the prophets" (Amos 3:7). Then God issues a call to "prepare to meet your God" (Amos 4:12). God mercifully gives opportunity for people to prepare for divine appointments.

The "observable" and visible kingdom or rule of God was anticipated in the first coming of the rule of God in Jesus Christ. In mercy God wants people prepared for His all-encompassing sovereign rule and thus He has sent His Son to prepare the way. So great is His mercy and kindness that He even sent John the Baptist to prepare the way of the One who prepares the way! _The kingdom is "now/not yet" for a very practical purpose—proper preparation!_ And this preparation means actual participation, at least in part, of all the blessings that will characterize God's kingdom at its future consummation. The "first course" of the "menu" of the great marriage supper of the Lamb is now available!

Forgiveness, peace, joy, healing, freedom, and love are ours now in anticipation of the coming glory of God's kingdom rule.

KINGDOM EXTRA

When will God's kingdom rule come about? Jesus used the analogy of a woman in labor in Matthew 24:8 where the word "sorrows" is literally the word for "labor pains." Anticipating His coming notes events that like labor pains can tell us the "birth" (His Coming) is imminent, but they cannot tell us the time of the birth. An increase in both the intensity and rapidity of the labor pains will signal the end of this age and the birth of the age to come just as increased labor pains indicate the end of pregnancy and the birth of a child. Therefore, we best be "about the Father's business" as we await the end of the age, for He alone knows when the "baby" will be born! For further study on this matter of the time of prophetic consummation, you may wish to consult such books as *Dreams, Visions and Oracles: the Laymen's Guide to Biblical Prophecy*, edited by Carl E. Armerding and W. Ward Gasque (Baker, 1977); *The Blessed Hope*, by George E. Ladd (Eerdmans, 1956), and *Armageddon Now!* by Dwight Wilson (Baker, 1977).

LET'S PUT IT ALL TOGETHER!

We have seen that the message of the kingdom is two-edged and relates to two frames of *time*:

First, God, in Christ, is *now* recovering man from his double loss—relationship *with* God and of rulership *under* God. He promised this at man's Fall, illustrated it in the patriarchs and Israel's history, and *now* the King has come to begin fully bringing it about. The kingdom is being realized *presently*, in partial and personal ways, as it is spread *through* all the earth by the Holy Spirit's power in the church.

Second, the kingdom will be realized *finally* in consummate and conclusive ways only at the return of Jesus Christ and by His reign *over* all the Earth. What we experience of His triumph now, in part, will then be fully manifest (1 Cor. 13:9, 10; 15:24; Rev. 11:15). This complete view allows for our understanding and applying the principles of "kingdom come" without falling into the confusion of expecting *now* what the Bible says will only be *then*. In the next chapter, we will study more of the prophetic word in relationship to the kingdom.

FAITH ALIVE

Do you have a situation in your life where you are wrestling with the dual tension of the "now/not yet" presence of the kingdom? In what ways can you manifest hope in the Lord while experiencing problems and setbacks in your current situation?

PROPHECY AND THE KINGDOM

Lesson 12

THE BIG IDEA

Why study the kingdom of God? So we can experience it! Let's discover how the certainty of God's future kingdom affects kingdom living today!

WHY STUDY PROPHECY?

Promise and prophecy are abundant in the Bible. God gives many assurances of His readiness to bless and often speaks of things He plans to do in the future. In both cases there are always conditions—God's call to align with His will so His word of promise can bless the obedient.

The purpose of predictive prophecy in the Bible is to teach, to warn, and to instruct toward obedience and fruitful living. It is never given to arouse curiosity or promote guesswork. In Matthew 24 Jesus makes several prophecies about things to come but tells His disciples that His purpose is essentially to elicit practical responses of obedient living (v. 42), not guessing at the possible schedule of forthcoming events (v. 36). Predictive prophecies also undergird our confidence in God's sovereignty and omniscience—that He is in control and that He *does* know the end from the beginning. But prophecy has never been given to cultivate passivity, as though it were a fatalistic statement from God. He has given prophecy to cultivate anticipation, faithfulness, trust, and obedience, not the presumption that "everything is over and done with."

◈ What did Jesus say was the purpose of His telling His followers about things that were to come? (John 13:19; 16:4)

_____

_____

FAITH ALIVE

Is there an area of your life where you face uncertainty or fear of the future? Take that area to God; rest in the confidence that He is a loving God who knows what is going to happen to you.

THE COMING KING AND KINGDOM
(Dan. 2, 7)

With the understanding that the purpose of prophecy is to lead us to obedient and confident trust in God, let's briefly study what the Bible has to say about His coming kingdom.

In the last lesson, we studied the now/not yet tension of the kingdom. We said that there are two comings at two moments of history. In this study guide, we have focused at length on the First Coming of the Messiah who came as the Lamb of God, the suffering Servant, to take away the sins of the world. We have learned about the dynamics of His kingdom rule—Holy Spirit power, worship, prayer, character, conflict, and kingdom heritage. But there is also a time when Jesus Christ will come in triumphant glory in fulfillment of the Scriptures.

We will now focus on the future coming of the kingdom spoken of by Daniel. Through prophetic vision, God revealed to Daniel that human kingdoms were going to be replaced by His eternal kingdom. The second chapter of Daniel describes a "great image"; chapter seven describes four "great beasts." The matter of interpreting these various kingdoms has led to diverse opinions. However, the bottom line is that Daniel points to a coming day when God's kingdom will prevail and all rival kingdoms will be destroyed.

Before answering the questions, read Daniel 2:31–45 and 7:1–27.

◇ What did Daniel say about the coming kingdom "which shall never be destroyed"? (Dan. 2:44)

_____

_____

◇ What happens to the stone that strikes the image? (Dan. 2:35)

_____

_____

◈ Turn to Daniel 7:13, where "One like the Son of Man" from heaven brings God's everlasting kingdom. (Remember that Jesus often used "Son of Man" to describe Himself.) What happens in Daniel 7:14?

_____

_____

◈ Who ultimately will possess the kingdom? (Dan. 7:18, 22).

_____

_____

Fully understanding these passages requires further study, but the basic fact remains: God's kingdom is coming, and it will last!

KINGDOM EXTRA

Dig into the text to compare the four parts of the "great image" in Daniel 2 with the "four great beasts" in Daniel 7. What do the descriptions suggest about the nature and strength of these kingdoms?

◈ Head of gold—first beast like a lion with eagle's wings (2:32; 7:4)

_____

_____

◈ Chest and arms of silver—second beast like a bear with ribs in its mouth (2:32; 7:5)

_____

_____

◈ Belly and thighs of bronze—third beast like a leopard with four wings (2:32; 7:6)

_____

_____

◈ Legs of iron, feet of iron and clay—fourth beast, strong and terrible with iron teeth (2:33; 7:7)

_____

_____

◈ Describe any kind of progression you see in the descriptions of these kingdoms.

_____

_____

_____

"POSSESS" THE KINGDOM!
(Dan. 7:18–27)

Daniel's prophecy in chapter 7 not only spans the spiritual struggle covering the ages through Messiah's First and Second Coming, but it uses two terms important to perceiving the biblical truth of the kingdom of God: "*dominion*" and "*possess.*"

"Dominion" (from Chaldee, *shelet*, "to govern, prevail, dominate") is in the hands of world powers (Dan. 7:6, 12) until the Coming of the Son of Man, at which time it is taken by Him forever (vv. 13, 14). But an interim struggle is seen between the First and Second Coming of Messiah. During this season, the saints "possess" (Chaldee, *chacan*, "to hold on" or "to occupy") the kingdom. This communicates a process of long struggle as the redeemed ("saints") "possess" what they have "received" (v. 18).

The scenario reads: (1) After the "judgment was made in favor of the saints" (a forecast of the pivotal impact of Christ's Cross upon which hinged both man's redemption and his reinstatement to the potential of his rule under God), an extended struggle ensues. (2) This struggle is described as the "time [which] came for the saints to possess the kingdom." They do battle against sinister adversaries and experience a mix of victories and apparent defeats (Dan. 7:25).

The prophecy from Daniel unveils the present age of the kingdom, which is one of ongoing struggle—with victory upon victory for the church. Yet it withholds its conclusive triumph until Christ comes again.

◈ From what have you just read, what is the meaning of the word "dominion"?

_____

_____

_____

◈ What is the meaning of "possess"? What are the implications of this for those who await their Lord's return?

_____

_____

Daniel's prophecy in chapter 7 also balances the question of divine sovereignty and human responsibility.

1. God's *sovereignty* accomplishes the foundational victory (v. 22) and in the Cross achieves the decisive victory allowing the saints new dimensions for advance and conquest.

2. God entrusts the *responsibility* for that advance to His own to "possess the kingdom," entering into conflict with His adversaries, at times at the expense of their apparent defeat (v. 26).

3. However, movement toward *victory* is theirs as they press the "judgment" of the "court" (vv. 22, 26) and seize realms controlled by evil. They wrestle the dominion from hellish powers, continuing in warfare until the ultimate seating of the Son of Man (vv. 14, 27).

◈ During the period where world powers have dominion, what are the saints to do? What have you learned from Daniel that can help you answer this?

_____

_____

◈ Whose responsibility is it to "possess the kingdom"? In what practical ways can the church advance God's kingdom?

_____

_____

_____

Prophetic systems vary as to how and when these words unfold on the calendar of church history, for the passage is subject to different schemes of interpretation, each with different projected chronologies. But the foundational fact remains that an agelong struggle between "the saints" and the power of evil in the world calls each believer to a commitment to steadfast battle, a mixture of victories with setbacks, and a consummate triumph anticipated at Christ's coming. In the meantime, we "receive" the kingdom and pursue victories for our King, by His power, making intermittent gains—all of which are based on "the judgment" achieved through the Cross.

◈ Turn to the New Testament. What is promised to those who endure? (2 Tim. 2:11, 12)

_____

_____

◈ What ultimately will happen? (Rev. 12:10, 11)

_____

_____

THE KINGDOM IN REVELATION

The Book of Revelation is an unfolding revelation of Christ's lordship. The writer John was given four significant visions when he was "in the Spirit" (Rev. 1:10; 4:2; 17:3; 21:10). These visions reveal the progressive unveiling of Christ's lordship over the church (chs. 1—3), over history (chs. 4—16), over all other lords (chs. 17—20), and over all creation (chs. 21: 22). Within this grand panorama of the rightful restoration of God's rule over His creation is the coming of His kingdom at the end of human history in the return of Christ to earth (Rev. 19).

Various interpretive systems see the events in Revelation occurring at different times within redemptive history. The mixture of pre-, a-, and post-millennial viewpoints has often fragmented the church, rather than providing a common base of wisdom for each group to receive while embracing one another as, presently, we all face a common adversary (Rev. 12:9). Seeing that no complete interpretive scheme will be verified until after Christ comes, our wisdom is to embrace the Cross as our salvation and our source of overcoming victory.

Let's seek to glean truth from the fascinating events foretold in Revelation.

◈ What will happen to the kingdoms of this world? (11:15)

_____

◇ What will happen to the devil? (20:10)

◇ What is coming? (21:1–3)

With the coming of God's eternal kingdom in the new heaven and earth, His eternal covenant now finds its grand fulfillment. God's solemn promise to restore headship, relationship and fellowship to a fallen race is now a reality. What was lost in the fall of Adam and Eve is not only regained but also transcended in the New Jerusalem.

◇ What will replace the "curse" that Adam and Eve brought upon themselves and the human race? (Rev. 22:3)

◇ Turn back to Revelation 21:3. Write what is said concerning the three dimensions of God's eternal covenant—restored *headship*, restored *relationship*, and restored *fellowship*.

◇ What will happen to tears, death, sorrow, crying, and pain? (21:4)

◇ Amazing words proceed from God's throne in Revelation 21:5. What are those words?

Not only is the old covenant fulfilled in the New Covenant, the New Covenant is now fully consummated. God's dwelling is now with His people, fully. God's people now include all peoples as the "nations ... walk in its light" (Rev. 21:24).

◇ How will "kings of the earth" respond to God's kingdom? (Rev. 21:24)

It is important to see that the New Jerusalem completely transcends the Garden of Eden. Note the surpassing description of the

New Jerusalem in Revelation 22:1-5 and compare it with what is said about the Garden of Eden in the second and third chapters of Genesis. The difference is not only in scope, but also in kind. Not merely do a man and wife have access to the Tree of Life, but nations will! Not only do they hear God's voice, but also His people will see His face. In God's eternal kingdom, His people will serve Him, see His face, and reign forever and ever (Rev. 22:3-5).

This is humankind's destiny. This is why we were created in God's image. This is why God redeemed our fallen race. We were redeemed to see and know Him—to serve and worship Him—to rule and reign with Him.

HOW TO POSSESS THE KINGDOM
(Matt. 24:14)

What can we do while waiting for the Lord's coming kingdom? We can be about His kingdom business! (Luke 19:13.)

In this study guide, we have studied the essential background of God's kingdom. His creative sovereignty, redemptive love, and seeming silence have prepared the way for us to understand and appreciate the significance and necessity of His kingdom rule. With the Coming of Jesus Christ, a time of promised fulfillment arrived (Mark 1:15). We were called to repentance—to turn fully from self-sufficiency and humbly trust Jesus Christ, God's Son, who died and rose to bring salvation to humankind. We were encouraged to enter His kingdom and do His work, preaching the Good News of His salvation to the world.

Jesus taught that there is an essential sign that must happen before the end times. He prophesied this in Matthew 24:14. Turn to this passage.

◈ What must happen?

◈ What will be preached?

◈ Where will it be preached?

◈ Then what will come?

Note that verse 14 says the gospel will be preached "in all the world [the inhabited earth] . . . to all the nations," (nations, *ethne*, means "ethnic/cultural groups"). This is the only sign that appears to have a "conditional element" of human responsibility within it. In other words, the end will come when Christ's last commission to make disciples of all nations is completed.

Now, until He returns, we are to do His kingdom work—to occupy the territory He has given us, being His representatives in a fallen world. Remember earlier in this lesson that you studied verses in Daniel that said the saints are to "possess" the kingdom? We are to become acquainted with the King, our lives aligned with His purposes. We are to take the message of salvation to all peoples of the world. As we do, we are to be filled with His Spirit, be formed by His character, pray to, and worship Him. We will experience the reality that the *presence* of the kingdom at this time calls each believer to responsible spiritual warfare and anticipated victories.

Dear friend, may you do battle in faith and with faithfulness. As you look to that day of His ultimate kingdom, know the Holy Spirit is preparing *you* for kingdom victories *today*!

FAITH ALIVE

In what ways can you "do the Lord's business" until He comes? What promises from the Word assure you of victory as you do His kingdom work?

Appendix A

OLD TESTAMENT BACKGROUND OF THE KINGDOM

The history of the human race dramatically underscored the need for "God's kingdom to come and His will to be done on earth as it is in heaven." Man's Fall and his sinful refusal to trust and obey his Creator brought only chaos, confusion, and destruction. Yet, hope emerged of a coming King who will bring His kingdom.

In chapters 9 (Genesis) and 10 (Heritage) you learned:

1. God is the Creator and Sustainer of all creation.
2. God made all things "good," especially man, whom He made in His own image and gave dominion over the earth.
3. Man succumbed to the Serpent's temptation and thereby lost his right to rule on God's behalf.
4. The "wages of sin is death"—both spiritual and physical. Man lost relationship and fellowship with God because he did not trust and obey his Creator. And so death characterized the race as humankind continued in unbelief and disobedience.
5. Most important, God had a "rescue plan." Sin was not the last word. Rather, it became the beginning point of God's redemptive love.
6. Abraham, the "father of faith," believed God and it was accounted to him for righteousness. He is God's revealed example of His plan to eventually reestablish His kingdom's rule in all the earth through people of His covenant.
7. God's call had been for Israel to become a "kingdom of priests and a holy nation."

8. But His people never seemed to be able to shake their idolatrous ways, though they were blessed by covenant relationship with God Himself. They broke God's covenant. They violated His Law. They refused God's prophets. They rejected His rule.

9. Instead of being a "light to the nations," God's people became like the nations and God sent them into captivity—Israel fell captive to Assyria; later Judah to Babylon.

10. True to His word that He would raise up an everlasting kingdom through the house of David (1 Sam. 7:16), God was faithful to bring back a remnant of His people to Jerusalem to rebuild the temple and reinstitute worship to the living God.

11. The people made reforms and attempted to follow the Law. But this did not bring God's presence or justice. They needed more! They needed the Deliverer promised to them by the prophets.

12. A long, dry, spiritual period followed. This must have been a time of disappointment and despair. Yet it was a time of anticipation and hope. It was a time of significant and necessary preparation for the promised Coming of God's King and His kingdom. The stage was set for the arrival of Jesus Christ.

Appendix B

THE CHURCH, ISRAEL, AND THE KINGDOM—WHERE DO YOU FIT?

The church at its inception was virtually entirely Jewish, and it remained so until the gospel began to spread. Ultimately the gospel spread to Antioch—where the first Gentile congregation began—the base from which the gospel spread into all the world.

In the Book of Romans, chapters 9 through 11, the apostle Paul deals with the question of the Jews in God's providence and purpose. These three chapters virtually stand alone, within the whole of the Bible, as an elaboration of the theology of God's dealing with the Jews. The Jews were the "firstfruit," the first people (through Abraham) to understand a covenant God. They then relayed the riches of that truth to the world, and through their agency, the Messiah came into the world. The Word of God calls Jews the "root," and the Gentiles are grafted-in branches. We're reminded that "because of unbelief, they [natural branches] were broken off, and you stand by faith. Do not be haughty, but fear. For if God did not spare the natural branches, He may not spare you either." When the fullness of the Gentiles is completed, "all Israel will be saved" (Rom. 11:16–27).

We are living in a sobering moment in history that calls us, as believers in Jesus Christ, to take a stand with Israel. We could be people of the last hour. We are not to be passive in the face of prophecy; we are called to pray with passion, to intercede, and to minister according to the words of the Savior who said it is not our task to speculate when the end will be. It is our responsibility to do kingdom business until He comes (Luke 19:13).[1]

KINGDOM EXTRA

What is God saying today to the church about Israel? Students desiring in-depth answers may consult the New Spirit-Filled Life Bible for a nine-article treatise, "Understanding Messianic Jewish Ministry" (Thomas Nelson, 2002, p. 1874-82). Topics include:

1. The Great Debate of the Apostles: Must a Gentile who believes in Yeshua, Messiah of Israel and King of the Jews, himself or herself become a Jew? (Acts 15)
2. The Abrahamic Covenant: What is its meaning and status as it relates to present-day Israel? (Gen. 12:2, 3)
3. God Is the God of Ishmael: How do Abraham's children of Arab tradition fit into God's covenanted purposes for Israel and the Jews? (Gen. 17:18)
4. God's Covenant Through Isaac and Jacob: What are the scriptural grounds for affirming God's distinct and special covenant with Abraham's descendants? (Gen. 26:1-5)
5. Abrahamic Covenant and Mosaic Covenant: To see how these two separate covenants differ is to begin to understand a mistaken conclusion drawn by some who doubt God's continuing and distinct purposes for Israel as a people and nation. (Gal. 3:17, 18)
6. The role of the believing Gentile in relationship to the unbelieving Jew today. (Rom. 11:11-24)
7. The prophesied spiritual restoration of Israel through a national revival. (Jer. 31:31-37)
8. Understanding the spiritual enrichment of the nations of the earth through the failure of Israel. (Rom. 11:11-15)
9. What might the comparison of today's non-Jewish believers with Acts 15's Jewish believers contribute to our vision for the future? (Acts 15:1-32)

FAITH ALIVE

Today many in Christ's corporate body are discovering the Old Testament and New Testament scriptures coming alive, moving their prayer, action, and outreach in behalf of the lost sheep of Israel. Praise God for this—yet another sign of the Holy Spirit ushering the church toward the coming of our Lord.

May faith fill our hearts for an outpouring of God's Spirit over the land of Israel and in her people. Before us, like never before, is a call to intercession.

[1] From Jack W. Hayford's "Why Stand with Israel Today?" (Living Way Ministries, 2002).